D1465692

TRAGÉDIE BOUFFE

RENÉ ARNAUD

Tragédie Bouffe

A Frenchman in the First World War

Translated by
J. B. Donne

LONDON
SIDGWICK & JACKSON

Originally published in French as *La Guerre 1914–1918: Tragédie Bouffe*

Copyright © 1964 Éditions France-Empire

This translation © 1966 Sidgwick and Jackson

Printed in Great Britain by
Cox and Wyman Ltd., London, Fakenham, and Reading for
Sidgwick and Jackson Ltd
1 Tavistock Chambers, Bloomsbury Way, London, W.C.1

CONTENTS

I

MY FIRST COLONEL

I KNOCKED timidly on the door of the building at the end of the farmyard, beyond the dung-heap.

'Come in!' roared a stentorian voice.

I opened the door, and my friend Guiganton and I entered. The Colonel was sitting near the window, in the light of a weak paraffin-lamp. We clicked our heels and stood perfectly at attention with our right hands stiff and quivering at the peaks of our kepis. Our kepis were dark blue, like our uniforms. It was January 1915, and the red uniforms of the pre-war days had been withdrawn after the battles of August and September 1914 had shown that red makes an excellent target— a fact that could have been discovered earlier, during the army manœuvres. In the same way the brand-new gold braid on our cuffs could have been turned back so as not to give us away to the German snipers.

'Good God!' thundered the Colonel. 'They're sending us babes-in-arms now!'

I was twenty-one, Guiganton was perhaps nineteen, but neither of us looked more than sixteen. After the terrible blood-baths of Morhange, Charleroi, the Marne and the 'Race to the Sea', our infantry regiments were short of officers. We had been called up at the beginning of September 1914, and in three months we had been turned into 2nd Lieutenants. Our instructor, who had himself been an officer cadet at the Military Academy of Saint-Cyr when war broke out and had been wounded in the arm at Charleroi, spent most of his time teaching as the difficult art of attaching the bayonet to the rifle to the command 'Fiiiix . . . bay'nets!', and the even more difficult one of replacing it in its scabbard ('Replaaaace . . . bay'nets!'). Pretty slim preparation for making war. But we were full of fervour and enthusiasm. Our only fear was that the war might end too soon, before we had even had time to reach the front. How humiliated we would have been to miss the great adventure of our generation! And then again, the glory of war will always appeal to lads of twenty.

We introduced ourselves. The Colonel told us to be seated, and then roared out:

'Butcher!'

The Colonel's batman hurried into the room. His name was Nauleau, which is common enough in the Vendée, but the Colonel never called him anything but the Butcher, for he enjoyed playing the old warhorse and no doubt it amused him to recall Nauleau's sanguinary peacetime occupation.

'For God's sake, Butcher, you bugger, bring us an apéritif! These two children are too young to drink absinthe, by God! Give them a St Raphael, and I'll have my usual. Hurry up, you old bastard, you old bastard, you!'

These 'terms of endearment' were pronounced on two different notes, the first rising sharply, the second falling like an echo of the first.

While the Butcher was arranging the bottles and glasses on the table we had leisure to take in our new chief. He was a huge man, but it was his

2

head that most attracted our gaze. He had a double chin and triple folds at the back of his neck, flabby red cheeks and big blue goggling eyes like a toad, which fixed on us a gloomy and disturbing look, and thin red hair, closely cropped, which one could scarcely see for he always kept his kepi on—a tall red kepi with a dirty blue cap-band, doubtless the sign of the 'Blue Side' at some former army manœuvres.

While we timidly sipped our St Raphaels, the Colonel took his absinthe strictly according to the prescribed rules. The green liquid filled the bottom of the glass, a perforated spoon was placed on the rim, sugar was put in the spoon, and from time to time water was poured on the sugar, which dissolved like melting snow. As the Colonel drank down this mixture he topped it up with neat absinthe. We found out later that, though absinthe was prohibited, the Colonel had managed to get hold of a nice little stock which was carefully stowed away in a trunk in one of the carts of the regimental transport. And so every day at noon and again at seven in the evening he was able to enjoy his favourite apéritif, just as he had done before the war at the Café des Mille Colonnes or the Café du Commerce.

His language was as colourful as his person. Besides his oaths and insults he frequently punctuated his conversation with a loud 'Pouff', blowing through his pouted lips in a way that reminded one of another sound, and even more often raised his hand in salute. Turning to us, he said:

'You're having dinner with us. Now, I'm a simple fellow. If I were by myself, I'd just have soup, vegetables and a bit of cheese for dinner . . . Pouff! That'll do me.' Here he gave a salute.

'But at your age, by God! you've got to have something more solid than that. But don't you worry, here at the front you'll have beef with every meal, by God! These commissariat buggers have never heard of anything but beef! Pouff! Enough to put you off the stuff for the rest of your life!' (Another salute.)

After that, while the Butcher was laying the table, he got up and announced, 'Well, lads, I'm going to have a pee!' We then saw that this vast man was still agile, despite his obesity. His legs were enormous, and yet he stepped lightly, like an elephant. They were confined in soft leather leggings laced up the sides—he would never have been able to put on a pair of boots, let alone get them off. On his shoulders he had the short dark blue cape which was then worn on top of the cavalry cloak, and this floated over his fat belly and strong thighs like an awning.

Through the door, which he had left open, we heard a cascade falling on the dung-heap, and another sound which this time did not issue from his mouth. On returning he said with a large smile, by way of excuse:

'I can never touch the hour-hand without making the clock strike, by God!'

As it was now dinner-time the regimental staff began to arrive: the adjutant, nervous and fidgety; the ensign, a greying, solemn, doleful man from Corsica; the senior medical officer, who was forever scratching his thick black beard; the quartermaster, who looked like a peaceable clerk from a government office; and finally the commander of the battalion to which I was to be attached, a small pallid man with a brown beard and a sugary nasal voice, who had also just joined the regiment.

They all appeared to be at least forty. To us they seemed old men.

We sat down at table and everyone began talking. Naturally we discussed the war, and the quiet sector of the Somme where the regiment had been immobilized in the trenches since the Race to the Sea in October 1914. There was also talk of the shelters dug beneath the snow-covered earth of the front line.

As the Butcher was serving the *bœuf bourguignon* we heard the Colonel's voice raised above those of the other guests, who one after the other fell silent:

'So the General said to me, "Magnier, I count on you and your battalion to take Hill 303!" "Pouff! sir," I said to him [here the Colonel saluted], "that's a tall order." "I count on you," he repeated. We set out, by God! One company in advance, one covering our left flank . . . Pouff! Two hours later, 303 was taken!' (Another salute.)

'But tell me, sir,' said the battalion commander, 'was this during the period of open warfare and the Race to the Sea last October?'

'Good God, of course not! It was during the army manœuvres in the south-west in 1913!'

That an officer should still be recounting his achievements at army manœuvres after six months of war and at scarcely a mile from the front line was really outrageous. No doubt we were all stunned by this superb example of warped professionalism, for after this remark 'an angel passed overhead' and nothing was heard but for the scraping of knives and forks on the plates.

If the Colonel drank his absinthe twice a day, if, wearing a kepi with a blue cap-band, he still talked about the army manœuvres, it was because for him the war was after all a continuation of garrison life with scarcely any change. The fact that the rifles now fired real bullets and the guns real shells did not affect him, for he never set foot in the front line and hardly ever moved beyond his command post. But he thoroughly enjoyed the pleasures of a pre-war commander. He was proud of his stentorian voice. The day after our arrival he was to confer the Cross of the Legion of Honour on our Commanding Officer, and that evening he said to him:

'My God! You'll see! When I say, "In the name of the President of the Republic . . .", pouff! they'll hear me at the other end of the village . . .'

What pleasure he must have taken in bawling out at inspections, 'Slope arms!' or 'Order arms!' It must have been ecstasy for him to watch hundreds of men moving all together at his word of command.

He also enjoyed the absolute power which the war gave him—but without ever abusing it. He had issued strict orders that all army drivers should pass through the village at walking pace. One fine evening a horse was heard at the trot. It was a gunner who had 'requisitioned' a little dog-cart from some château or other and was bringing back food and drink from Amiens for the officers' mess. He was passing through the village at a spanking pace, probably despising us poor bloody infantry, when he suddenly saw the dark form of our Colonel appear beside the road, his stick held high and his cape streaming in the wind.

'Halt, you son of a bitch! Halt! By God! I'll have you shot!'

6

The terrified gunner heaved on the reins and stopped dead. The Colonel continued in a somewhat milder tone:

'So, a bloody gunner doesn't give a damn for regulations? You go through this village at a walking pace, next time, my God! or I'll have you shot! Now, bugger off, but make it a walk!'

A few months later the Colonel had his headquarters at Bronfay Farm, north of Bray-sur-Somme. The farm was only shelled when the transport passed it on the way to the front line, and the sentry on duty at the entrance had strict instructions to forbid all vehicles from passing. One fine evening in May the Colonel was sitting at a table at the bottom of the farmyard, drinking his absinthe, while the faithful Butcher, standing in the middle of the yard, was describing the flight of one of our aeroplanes which was being chased by the white puffs of enemy shells behind the farm and outside the Colonel's range of view. Suddenly two light lorries were heard, rather than seen, to flash like a pair of arrows past the entrance. They were a couple of Red Cross Ford ambulances driven by two of those American volunteers who had rushed over to take part in the war back in 1915 as if it were a gigantic base-ball game. They clearly wanted to visit the front at Carnoy and were bent on getting as near as possible in their vehicles. The Colonel's face turned from red to violet in a moment, and with an oath he called the duty sergeant.

The sergeant hurried forth. He was a small man called Chacun, with lively eyes and a satyr's beard. He froze to attention six paces from the Colonel. The Colonel cast a withering look at him and yelled:

'For God's sake, Sergeant! You know your orders?'

'Yessir.'

'And your men? Are they all asleep? You blithering idiot, I'll have you shot!'

'Yessir.'

'Shut up!'

'Yessir.'

'For God's sake are you going to shut up?'

'Yessir.'

The Colonel's face turned from violet to black, and I thought he was going to have a stroke. He must have thought so too, for he made a visible effort to control himself. With a wave of his hand he dismissed the sergeant—who had had the last word—and so the matter was allowed to drop. For this great 'bawler out', as the men described him, who was always talking about shooting people, would doubtless have been very upset to have had to pronounce a death sentence at a court-martial. He shouted often but he hardly ever punished. In place of punishment he preferred castigation in public by means of the daily 'orders' which were stencilled and distributed to all companies, and which, when we were not in the trenches, had to be read out in front of the assembled men. This is how he poured shame on a soldier who had complained to the visiting General of a shortage of bread:

'Assuming that this blackguard has not enough bread, the Colonel is absolutely certain that he has enough money in his pocket to spend on wine and to imbibe it in excessive quantities. His face is clear evidence of this. Such facetiousness is in bad taste and the sign of a bad soldier. . . . It shows a real lack of appreciation of what the quartermaster is doing for you, to tell tales that make one yawn one's head off just in order to be the centre of attention and to be able to say afterwards, "There, you see, I wasn't afraid of speaking out to the General!" When the General left he said, "That soldier is absolutely useless. You can tell that by just looking at him." The five sous per day which the Government gives you is intended for spending on creature comforts—and that includes white bread.'

It was also by means of the daily 'orders' that he publicly censured a soldier for having complained to the General that his trousers were in bad condition. 'Our forefathers of the French Revolution had no need of trousers in order to win; that is why they were called Sans-Culottes!'

If he did not like punishing his men, he did not like rewarding them either. For months he refused to forward any recommendations for the Croix de Guerre. The backbiters said that he had no intention of giving to others a decoration that he did not hold himself. But the example of the other regiment in our brigade, in which the green and red ribbon was generously distributed, eventually decided him to do likewise.

While we were in Champagne in January 1916, my turn to go on leave came round. I was to go by train, together with another officer from the battalion, Captain Estève, who was thirty-four and had served fifteen years in Africa as an N.C.O. On the strength of my twenty-two years I called him in a friendly way 'old 'un', and he responded by calling me 'young 'un'. On the day of departure he said to me:

'Young 'un, before leaving let's go and pay our respects to the Colonel.'

9

'What's the point, old 'un? He doesn't give a fig for us.'

'Young 'un, you're wrong. You've read lots of books but you don't know life and you don't understand men. You'll find that the Colonel will be very touched. Come on.'

I let myself be persuaded and we went to the Colonel's headquarters. It lay at the bottom of a deep sap at Trou-Bricot, in a bleak countryside of pine woods and barren fields.

After receiving Estève the Colonel called me in and said:

'And where are you going on leave, for God's sake?'

'To Paris, sir.'

'To Paris? And what are the girls going to say?'

I did not know what to reply.

'Yes, what are they going to say if you haven't got anything up there?' and he pointed to the left side of my tunic, in the region of my heart. 'Go on, bugger off next door and get my secretary to help you find a suitable citation in the *Army Bulletin*!'

That is how I came to receive the Croix de Guerre and my first decoration. After having dreamed of being decorated in front of the troops, what a farce! At least I was sufficiently modest, when writing up my own citation inspired by the *Bulletin*, to avoid the usual bombast, 'did not hesitate' or 'had no fear', and to refer simply to my baptism of fire in which I felt I had done my job honourably.

For all his idiosyncrasies and shouting, this great coarse man was very popular with his soldiers.

First of all, they knew that his bark was harmless. Then, every day he attended personally to the catering, and the regiment had the reputation of being the best fed in the division. The Colonel was not a little proud of this and in his daily orders he did not fail to make malicious allusions to 'our men taking pity on the troops of certain regiments who come and beg food from them'. In this way he hit at the other regiment in our brigade, for, as is usually the case, the two regiments were not on good terms. 'My enemy is he who does as I do,' runs the Arab proverb—or is it Chinese?

The men also appreciated the offhand way in which the Colonel sometimes treated his immediate superiors. General Ninous, who commanded the brigade, was a small, spare man with a white moustache, who came from the Midi and proudly wore the green and black ribbon of the campaign of 1870–71. In 1915 he was therefore well over sixty. However, he was very active and often went to visit the front lines. When he arrived at the Colonel's command post the scene was comic. From the top of the ladder leading down to the deep dug-out where the Colonel had entrenched himself the General would call out in his strong southern accent:

'Magnier, are you coming with me to see the *poilus*?'

From the depths of his retreat the Colonel would reply in his thundering voice:

'You'll excuse me, sir, but pouff! I've spent the night doing the rounds of the sector' (of course he had not even set foot there) 'and pouff! I'm a bit exhausted this morning.'

Good old General Ninous never pressed the matter, but went off on his own to the front lines.

It was this General who one day decided to send an orderly to Colonel Magnier with the gift of a duck *pâté*. Now, the evening before we had eaten duck in the Colonel's mess. The latter questioned the orderly:

'A *pâté*? What sort of *pâté*?'

'A duck *pâté*, sir.'

'Duck? Pouff! You can tell the General where he can stuff his duck *pâté*!'

I do not know whether this repartee got back to the General, but it went the rounds of the regiment and did not fail to increase the Colonel's popularity.

But there was a further reason for this popularity, of a rather more dubious nature. We have remarked that the Colonel never went 'up the line'. The men did not hold this against him. They excused him on account of his obesity. 'That bastard Crouquougnious [that was his nickname], he couldn't get up the line. The old son of a bitch is far too fat to get through the communication trenches!' In a strange way they were grateful to him for this. For these reservists from the Vendée, mostly over thirty and nearly all with families, had little enthusiasm for fighting. They considered that the regiment was not intended for attack but only for defence, for holding a sector of trenches—and even then a quiet sector. They reckoned that with such a Colonel the High Command would avoid engaging them in a murderous assault. And they were right. As long as the Colonel was at the head of the regiment we went through all the operations, even the Champagne Offensive of 25th September 1915, without heavy losses. But a few weeks after the Colonel had been removed from his command the regiment was involved in the fighting at Verdun and lost three-quarters of its total strength.

One may wonder how this Colonel Blimp was able to retain his command for nearly two years. Doubtless he knew how to combine, to use one of his favourite expressions, the prudence of the serpent with the intelligence of the opossum. But he must also have had friends in high places. When General de Castelnau came to inspect the troops, after making a rather unoriginal speech about 'defending our native soil against the pillage, fire and violation of the Boches', he went on to speak of his personal regard for the Colonel. As Castelnau was, to use Clemenceau's phrase, 'a monk in boots', I came to the conclusion that the Colonel was well thought of by the bishops, although he was not a practising Catholic. But an officer of the Divisional General Staff whom I encountered in civilian life after the war, assured me that Colonel Magnier was one of those 'terrible Freemasons'. Perhaps he was clever enough to keep a foot in both camps.

Despite these connections, the day came when he was relieved of his command. It was in October 1915, the day after the Champagne offensive, in which our regiment had not achieved very much. We had held the trench on the right pivot of the attack and we had been the only regiment in the division not to go over the top. After this exploit, as we were resting in a village in the rear, the Colonel gathered the officers together in a farmyard in order to bid us farewell, and uttered a few hollow phrases about the regiment he was leaving to our care. Major Garnier, the senior officer, who had a jaundiced face due to a bad liver, was taking over command of the regiment and must have been overjoyed at the Colonel's departure, for he cordially detested him. He considered it was his duty to reply on behalf of the officers of the regiment. But he was no orator. After a few words he lost the thread of what he was saying, and broke down and sobbed, stammering, 'I can't go on . . . I can't go on . . .' Some professional soldiers are easily moved to tears. Perhaps these hardened old battleaxes are repressed sentimentalists at heart.

So the Colonel left. Thereafter we reoccupied a sector in the Bois d'Hauzy on the railway line between Sainte-Ménehould and Vouziers. The regimental headquarters was installed in the gatekeeper's cottage at a level-crossing. Despite his liver, Major Garnier drew merrily on the Colonel's canteen-cellar—which the latter had not taken with him—and on the stores of clean white paper: for he too liked to write out orders destined for his daily briefing, thinking no doubt that he would thus establish his authority as commanding officer.

The supplies arrived along the railway on flat, four-wheeled trolleys which in peacetime are used by men working on the line. These trolleys were drawn by mules, and the track alongside the line served as a tow-path.

One warm November evening Major Garnier was sipping his absinthe on his door-step, no doubt meditating on the text of the 'rocket' that would appear in the following day's 'orders', when he saw a large mule toiling round the next bend in the track. He was surprised, for it was not time for the stores to arrive; but a second later the Major's jaw dropped and his eyes started to pop. The mule was drawing a rope, the rope was drawing a trolley, on the trolley was a chair,

14

and in the chair, his hands resting on his vast thighs, sat the Colonel, who had managed, God knows how, to get reinstated and was returning to take up his command once more. As is customary in the army, where delicacy is a thing unheard of, Major Garnier had received no notification. His face turned from its usual yellow to green. The two men must have had a few stormy sessions when it came to accounting for the bottles of absinthe and reams of paper which had disappeared during the interregnum.

It was only several months later, just before our move up to Verdun, that Colonel Magnier's dismissal became finally effective.

In the wars of long ago, men boasted of the number of horses that had been killed *under* them. During the 1914–18 war, I had, though I do not boast of it, several colonels relieved of their command *over* me. But I have a soft spot for Colonel Magnier, ruddy-faced, gruff and yet well-meaning, who personified an army that has doubtless disappeared for ever.

II

HOW I, UNINTENTIONALLY, TOOK A PRISONER, AND MY FIRST ENCOUNTER WITH THE GENERAL STAFF

I HAD just 'gone up the line' for the first time and was in command of a company, replacing an officer killed the day before, when I unintentionally took a prisoner.

In this sector of the Somme our lines were dominated by the Haie-Noire, 400 yards away. This was a German strongpoint which was being continually strengthened, as we could tell by the new heaps of fresh earth which appeared every day. (In January 1915 the art of camouflage was still unknown.) The High Command decided to bombard these field-works. It was something of an event in this sector, in which the artillery on either side normally remained silent, doubtless in order to save ammunition. So, one fine afternoon the 95s of a Belgian armoured train near Albert and two French 120-mm. guns—an enormous calibre at this stage of the war—began to shell the Haie-Noire. Since the enemy made no reply we all stood in the trenches as if we were at the theatre, admiring the columns of brown earth thrown up by each explosion.

Suddenly, in between two bursts, we saw a figure bob up from the German fort and come running towards us. It was a Fritz who probably could not take it any longer and had decided to surrender. His officers and fellow-men were presumably sheltering underground and could see nothing, otherwise they would probably have fired on the deserter. From our side, one or two look-out men let loose a few rounds but fortunately missed. The shout went up, 'Don't shoot!', and the man was able to reach our lines safe and sound.

With his hands up he stumbled through the inadequate barbed wire, which was supposed to protect us, and jumped into our trench out of breath, a few yards from where I stood. He was of course without arms or equipment, but was wearing a verdigris greatcoat and a forage-cap with red piping and a flash. He was small, he had a hunted look, he was hollow-chested and he coughed pitifully, spluttering full in one's face. We had to wave him to stand back. His unshaven yellowish face, covered with reddish hair, was bathed in sweat. Before we had even asked him to, he emptied all his pockets: one would have thought that he had read up the behaviour of the perfect prisoner in the army manual in advance. I found from his pay-book that his name was Franz Sadecki. He began to explain in a mixture of French and German that he was Polish, that he was sick of the Germans, and he shouted, 'Kaiser *kaput*!' as evidence that he consigned the Emperor Wilhelm II to the devil.

The affair had its repercussions next day. If in this quiet sector a bombardment was an event, the capture of a prisoner was even more so. I had the honour of being visited by the General commanding the Army Corps. He was a small man whose

17

face was covered in eczema and acne. He had formerly been our Military Attaché in Athens and the story went that he had had his successes at the Greek court, but this seemed very unlikely in view of his physical appearance. At his side stood his A.D.C., a very handsome man with a satisfied smile, who was wearing a comforter. I gave him a black look: we had just received strict orders to forbid all men from wearing comforters, and I was still young enough to become indignant at seeing a bad example being set by those superiors who laid down the law and should have been the first to respect it. It was probably on this occasion that my hatred of General Staffs was born.

The General asked me what had happened the day before, so I told him.

'Young man,' he said, 'you have lost an excellent opportunity of winning the Legion of Honour. You had only to advance with your company to occupy the fort, which had been knocked to bits by our artillery, and to get a working party to connect it with our trenches. We would then have been in possession of an extremely useful observation post for our gunners.'

I was too new to the front to realize the enormity of these remarks. But I imagine that, as a mere 2nd Lieutenant, I would have been placed under arrest as a raving madman if I had taken such an initiative. To make a company advance in order to attack a position 400 yards from the French lines would have been an act of insanity. Since we were fighting a siege war, this would have been equivalent to making a sortie, occupying one of the besiegers' redoubts and connecting it to the walls of the town besieged—all this with only 120 men, the total strength of the company.

18

The German counter-attack would have quickly 'annihilated' us, to use the charming expression of their communiqués. And that is without mentioning the problems of maintaining contact with the companies on either flank and with the artillery.

That a general could make such a suggestion in January 1915 proved that he understood nothing about this new form of warfare and that he was still imbued with the doctrine of the out-and-out offensive, which was the official policy of the French army in 1914. Such complete lack of understanding explains the enormous number of ill-judged unsupported assaults made during the calamitious winter of 1914–15, in which we had lost so many men for nothing.

III

MY BAPTISM OF FIRE

OURS was one of the quietest sectors. When I had first 'gone up the line' it was under snow, and the white mantle hid or softened features and muffled sound, so that the lines which faced the enemy, and the boyaux running at right-angles to the trenches, which had already half fallen in and become too wide, looked like sunken roads zigzagging across a peaceful winter country-side. We lived in dug-outs built into the sides of either the advanced or communication trenches, whose roofs, level with the ground, were made of corrugated iron and sometimes a few short logs, covered with a thin layer of earth. We were therefore at the mercy of every German shell. But, as I have said, the enemy artillery was as silent as ours, and it was very rare to hear the 'Shooooo . . . Boom' of the German 77s. Water often trickled into these poor dug-outs, but we worked up a roaring fire in the stoves with wood 'borrowed' from the neighbouring village, without worrying about the smoke giving our position away to the enemy. Moreover, he did the same.

One ran hardly any risk except at certain look-out points, closely watched by snipers who did not fail to 'salute' you if you looked out too often. The bullets sounded like the crack of a whip and if they did not hit the loop-hole itself they struck the dry earth near by, sending up a little cloud of dust, or else planted themselves in a sugar-beet. Another risk: certain of the lines and communication trenches on a slope were subject to enfilading fire from a machine-gun post on the opposite side of the gully. This was how the Lieutenant whose place I had taken shortly after reaching the front, had been killed outright by a bullet through his head. This was the first war death that I had seen. I was not particularly affected by it. I had met him too recently to get to know him and strike up a friendship, and I was so full of life that it was impossible for me to imagine myself like him, lying on a stretcher with that detached air which the dead have. Moreover, was it not written that I should come back? In September 1914, as I was travelling by train from Paris to join my first regiment at Vannes, a journey which lasted three days, one of my travelling companions who had been born in Pondicherry and who imagined he had absorbed some of the knowledge of the fakirs with his ayah's milk, solemnly read in my face that I would 'come through', and despite my scepticism this prediction strengthened my confidence.

So I watched this corpse being borne away without seeing in it any portent for myself. His face and shoulders had been covered with canvas. On the stretcher his two outstretched legs in the dark blue dungarees which covered his red trousers, suddenly brought to my mind certain illustrations from a book of my childhood describing the battles of Napoleon. I saw once more the legs of soldiers killed at Montmirail and Champaubert, their heads and shoulders lying in a river. In those days these pictures had evoked in me I could not tell what dark pleasure.

It was much later that I discovered that the pleasure was a physical one, and that there is a mysterious connection between death and sensuality.

It was at this time that I attended my first burial at the front. After six days in the front line we spent six days in reserve at the Château de Bécourt, a country house which had suffered greatly from the bombardments. The library, where I liked to wander about, was on the north side and thus more exposed to the enemy fire, so that my wanderings were always spiced with danger. Afterwards I regretted that my scruples, which were then very strong, had forbidden me to 'borrow' a nice little edition of Sterne's *Sentimental Journey*, which must later have been destroyed. We slept in the cellars, whose walls were fully illustrated with pages cut out of *La Vie Parisienne*, pictures of good-time girls showing their thighs half sheathed in silk. We did not wait for the Americans to decorate our rooms with 'pin-ups'. It was in the grounds of the château that I saw a young Breton soldier from the 19th Regiment being buried. He had been killed by a grenade at La Boisselle, the next sector to ours. He lay on a stretcher, the top half of his body wrapped in canvas. Two men carried him to a shallow grave that they had dug hurriedly between bursts of gun-fire. But the body was not shovelled into the earth as if it were a dog's: a young soldier who had been following the other two passed a white surplice over his greatcoat and recited the prayers for the dead, finishing with a *Requiescat in pace*. Then the bearers slipped the body of this twenty-one-year old boy, who could perhaps speak hardly a word of French, off the stretcher into the grave. Although I had grown unfamiliar with religion, I was deeply moved by this simple endeavour to achieve a sense of holiness in the midst of the brutal realities of war.

All these deaths were little more than accidents. It was only a month and a half after my arrival at the front, on 28th February, that I received my baptism of fire in the front line.

As on every other day, I had had myself wakened while it was still pitch dark so as to make my rounds before dawn—dawn being the recognized time for raids and surprise attacks. In the darkness I went from one look-out to the next. Each one of them stood guard for two hours, with the patience of a hunter in his hide. These men of the Vendée were scarcely out of their element, for they were all hunters, not to say poachers. They had more experience than I had, and less imagination and nervousness. When I stopped at a firing-step to look out over no-man's-land, I sometimes mistook the stakes of our thin network of barbed wire for the silhouettes of a German patrol, knee to ground and ready to leap forth. I stared at the stakes, I saw them advance, I heard the greatcoats rubbing the earth and the jangling of bayonet scabbards . . . And then I turned towards the soldier on guard, and his equanimity reassured me. Since he saw nothing it meant there was nothing there—only my anxious hallucination.

A cold breath of air announced that day was about to break. I watched for the moment when the horizon would begin to pale and the lark climb above the trenches, wings beating in the morning sky. The outlines of the countryside were beginning to take form when I heard a shot,

23

quickly followed by others. In less than a minute the rifle-fire was general.

'Hurry up! Hurry up!' I ran to the next dug-out to wake the sleepers, but the men were already coming out, rifle in hand and buckling their packs on their backs. 'Get to your posts!' In the case of attack my section had the task of occupying an outwork recently dug to the plans of the Engineers, which left the front line trench and formed an arc in front of it. The General Staff, which always had the offensive in mind, wanted in this way to provide jumping-off points closer to the German lines. My men and I therefore had to defend this outwork, which was still little more than three feet deep, and which had of course been carefully pinpointed by the German artillery.

At that moment a glorious red rocket went up from the enemy lines and the curtain-fire was unleashed on our heads. Probably a commanding officer in front of us had panicked and thought that we were attacking. The 77s began to fall thick and fast in front of and behind our outwork and to deafen us with their whirrings and whinings and explosions. Shrapnel was flying everywhere, lurid as burning coals. The pungent smell of the cordite assailed our nostrils. My heart was thumping, I must have been white and I was trembling with fear. I lit a cigarette, feeling instinctively that this would help to calm my nerves. I noticed that the men were crouching at the bottom of the narrow trench, their heads under their packs, waiting for the barrage to end. No one was trying to see what was happening between the lines. It was possible that the German infantry were coming up behind their fire-curtain. It was even said that sometimes they advanced under

24

their own shells. Stepping over the men's backs I hurried to a bend I knew in the trench, from which one had an extensive view over the lines. From that moment my fear calmed down. Although my head was above the parapet I took no notice of the shells which were exploding in front and behind, nor of the shell-splinters which were spinning off in every direction. I no longer thought of the danger, I had eyes only for the slope that separated the two lines. I had become completely involved in the situation. My eyes searched no-man's-land and I behaved exactly as if I were certain that no shell or shrapnel could touch me. There was certainly nothing meritorious in this. As a simple soldier without any responsibility I would have been like the others, curled up in the bottom of the trench, wincing, thinking only of the next explosion which would perhaps blow me to pieces. But my concern with what had to be done freed me from fear. The true war hero is not the officer, for whom it is easy to forget the danger if he has the will to do his job, it is not the specialist—the machine-gunner, artilleryman or signaller, who can also forget the perils if he concentrates on carrying out his functions—the hero is the simple soldier without any special skill, who has only the rifle in his hand to keep his mind off the thought of death.

Little by little the storm of gun-fire calmed down. Two men had been killed in the neighbouring section, five in the company on our right. I heard later the explanation of this false alarm. Two of our look-outs had amused themselves by shooting at a flight of migrating birds, curlews perhaps, which were passing over our trenches.

This prank had been all that was necessary to spark off the rifle-fire and bombardment.

The French communiqué at 23.00 hrs. on 1st March 1915 gravely announced: 'At Bécourt, near Albert, a German attack has been completely checked by our fire.'

That is how history is written.

IV

MINE WARFARE

IN April we changed sector and a new kind of fighting was revealed to us—mine warfare.

The two lines as they had become established after the fighting at the time of the Race to the Sea, in October 1914, were sometimes very close to one another, separated by only a stone's throw of open ground. The Engineers then came to the rescue of the infantry by digging underground galleries out as far as the opposing trench, which they then blew up together with its defenders. Thereupon the infantry leapt forward to occupy the enormous crater formed by the explosion. In this way a few yards were gained and a communiqué announced this great success to the world. It was pretended that by this method 'artillery observation points were won'. In actual fact one could observe absolutely nothing from these craters because one was so close to the enemy that one could not show one's face without getting a bullet through one's head, nor raise a periscope without the glass being shattered. But the General Staff were unaware of such details, or did not want to know about them, and this insane warfare continued.

The infantry did not very much care for this new invention of the Engineers'. Besides the fact that occupying a crater cost men, each French mine called forth a retaliatory mine from the enemy, and it was a matter of who could blow up the other first. The look-outs feared not only a frontal attack, even more to be dreaded now that the enemy was so close, but in the silence of the night they held their ears to the ground and listened with a sinking heart to the regular thuds of the German sapper's pick as he worked like a mole underneath. In order to reassure the men I pointed out that there was no danger as long as one could hear the enemy at work. On the other hand, when one could hear him no longer it meant that he was in the process of tamping the mine and the explosion would come shortly. But meanwhile the company would doubtless be relieved and we would leave to our successors the honour of being blown up.

In fact, we were lucky enough to avoid the experience, and we had neither to blow anyone up and occupy a crater after the explosion, nor counter-attack to re-take a crater lost to the enemy. Our most dangerous exploit was to mount guard on a crater near Carnoy. Moreover, it would have been difficult for us to do otherwise. By way of reinforcements we had just been given some worthy Territorials from the Midi. They had all done their military service in 1891 or 1894—that is to say, they were at least forty years old—and they considered they had been put in the front line by mistake, since Territorials of their age should, they said, be guarding the railway lines in the rear or at the most occupying positions way back in the second line of defence. Nevertheless, they showed goodwill and quietly carried out my orders, youngster though I was, for they were twenty years older than me, since I had not been born or had only just been born at the time they were doing their military service.

The crater that we occupied was huge. A circular path had been made on the lip of the crater which enabled one to walk right round without being seen by the enemy. Look-outs were posted on the north edge, and on the south was Company Headquarters. The north edge was only two or three yards from the nearest German sentry, whom one could hear cough and whose bayonet one could see shining in the sunlight. In the pit of the crater the Engineers had started to dig a new tunnel in the direction of the enemy. One entered this on all fours, scratching oneself on the rough beams supporting the earthen roof, which was very loose as a result of the explosion.

This enormous crater, which was perhaps thirty yards in diameter, was the show-piece of the sector. Visitors came to see it every day from the neighbouring sectors, and countless photographs were taken. One of these appeared in an illustrated daily, *Excelsior*, now long defunct with a quite erroneous caption stating that this huge hole was due to the explosion of a German shell of very great calibre. I have a confused memory of one of these visitors, a sergeant of Engineers, with whom I chatted for a good two hours. We took an immediate liking to one another. Young men can sometimes strike up a sudden friendship in this way without any emotional undertones. We never saw one another again.

During our stay only one tragic episode occurred. After lunch one day the 2nd Lieutenant who commanded the company, the wine and spirits having gone to his head, suddenly had the idea of telephoning the gunners 'to send a few 75s to the bastards over there!' Sure enough, there was a battery watching over our crater, for a few seconds after the telephone call four angry shells whined over us so low that we instinctively ducked our heads. They burst abruptly with an excruciating noise and four clouds of black smoke leapt from the north edge of the crater where our lookouts were posted. We heard screams and groans. Half a dozen of our men had been terribly wounded in the legs by the explosion of the shells, which had fallen short. Several of the wounded were in fact our 'old' Territorials from Avignon and Narbonne. They wept like children.

The day after this incident an artillery officer came and explained to us that the sunlight had the effect of shortening the shells' trajectory. As a result of this incident we harboured an invincible distrust of gunners—a distrust that is borne by all infantrymen.

V

CORPSES IN THE SPRING

IN the good old days, when siege warfare was carried out by professional soldiers, a truce was agreed on after the battle in order to retrieve and bury the dead, for both sides feared the plague. Moreover, one did not wish the heroes' remains to be left exposed to the ravages of sun and rain. Perhaps it was also feared that the morale of the survivors would be shaken by the spectacle of the rotting corpses of their comrades-in-arms.

We have changed all that. In our wars nowadays, the entire population fights, and there is no more truce. In the 1914–18 War the corpses of fallen soldiers were left to rot between the lines. There was no question of asking for a suspension of hostilities. Whoever had done so would have aroused the suspicions of both sides. His own would have suspected him of wishing to fraternize with the enemy, and the enemy would have feared that the stretcher-bearers who entered no-man's-land to retrieve the dead, were in fact observers sheltering under the Red Cross and profiting from this unique occasion to leave the trenches and study the enemy's positions other than at ground level, or even perhaps troops preparing for a treacherous attack and concealing a machine-gun in a stretcher.

It was thus that, in the Carnoy sector in the

spring of 1915, we had to mount guard for several weeks a few yards from a line of corpses: eight or ten French soldiers mown down by a German machine-gun during one of those vain and senseless unsupported attacks in the winter of 1914–15, which had cost us so many men. They lay face downwards, a pace apart—the interval prescribed for assault troops in the pre-war tactical manuals.

I had plenty of opportunity to look at them during my rounds. In the radiant June dawn they gave off an unwholesome stench, against which the only recourse was a cigarette. While the spring sap mounted the boughs and branches, where branches and boughs still remained, the worms accelerated the work of decomposition and their wriggling played its part in the renewal of nature. I became quite familiar with the nearest corpse. Its right cheek was dissolving into a blackish liquid in the grass. Its arm still appeared to grasp the rifle whose bayonet had rusted. The dark blue of the greatcoat has turned to grey, and the belt and ammunition pouch had crumpled up under the snow and rain.

La Rochefoucauld wrote that one cannot gaze on death. Nevertheless we were forced to stare these decomposing corpses in the face, thinking inevitably that perhaps such would be our lot on the morrow. No doubt we had less pity for them than anxiety for ourselves. After all, their suffering had ended and they had been killed outright, felled like oxen in the slaughter-house. It might be our own fate to lie dying for hours or even days, with a bullet in the stomach or in the spine, and we had only a fleeting thought for the next-of-kin of the 'missing', who would have been driven insane on seeing what the war had done to their son, husband or lover.

And then, on returning from doing the rounds, one shook off these morbid thoughts and threw oneself on one's food with the appetite of a horse, as at those family meals following a country funeral. The feeling for life returned, one gorged oneself, drank, relished a glass of brandy, smoked a cigar, and thought no more of the corpses until the next round brought back before one's eyes that indefinable something that has no name in any language.

VI

RAILWAY TRANSPORT

TIDDLEY pom, tiddley pom, tiddley pom . . .
The rhythm of the train reminded me of
Greek anapaests—two shorts and a long—and
lulled me to sleep as we travelled through the
night in August 1915. We had been relieved in
the Somme by the B.E.F. Soldiers in khaki had
arrived bringing with them the aroma of cherry-
wood pipes and sweet tobacco. They played the
accordion to their heart's content, without worrying about calling the enemy's attention to the
relief, or attracting a few salvoes of 105s. The
previous year I had had to translate aloud a
passage of Ruskin, unseen, for an examination,
and now I wanted to speak English to show off my
knowledge. It was not a happy experience. The
British troops kept on talking of 'blankets', a word
I did not know. Ruskin no doubt had had no need
of it to describe the stones of Venice. It was only
after a while that I understood what it meant.
These regular soldiers, all excellently equipped,
were probably trying to get me to buy one of
their blankets so that they could visit the cafés
and the girls on the proceeds.

So we travelled on. Day broke. Ours was the
regulation military train with twelve flat trucks
loaded with vehicles and forty cattle-trucks bearing the inscription in white letters which so
amused our American allies when they arrived in

France: Men 36–40; Horses (lengthways) 8. There were about thirty men in each truck, some sprawling on the straw, others sitting at the open door with their legs dangling, watching the countryside and smoking their pipes. In the centre of the train was the only passenger coach, an old first-class carriage with four or five compartments, very high on the wheels, with neither corridor nor toilets, and reserved for the officers. Whether in war or peace, a railway journey really makes one aware of class inequality. In the trenches my dug-out scarcely differed from that of the men, and indeed we often had a dug-out in common. Here, on the train, it was a far cry from our first-class seats to the cattle-trucks of our men.

However, they hardly cared. They were as happy as schoolboys on holiday, and their only thought was to take advantage of the next stop to stock up on wine. At every station that we passed through sympathetic civilians standing behind the barrier offered wine to the 'poilus'. It was their way of 'contributing to the final victory', and above all of expressing their feelings for the fighting man. As soon as the train stopped, the soldiers swept out towards their benevolent providers like a flight of swallows.

The Major was roused by this disorder. He forbade the men to leave their trucks. But try and forbid Frenchmen—above all those from the Vendée—to drink good wine, especially when it is free! At the next stop, the same scene. The Major leapt on to the platform, red with rage. He called on the men to explain themselves, but they avoided him. Choking with fury, he succeeded in seizing one of the culprits who was returning in triumph with his canteen filled. The Major snatched the flask and, mad with rage, poured the wine out on to the station platform, muttering, 'There now!' The civilians behind the barrier murmured. The men were furious with this sacrilegious waste—for to them wine is something more holy than bread. This is, no doubt, the way in which mutinies sometimes arise.

Where were we going? We did not know. Various rumours came from the cook-house, for the field-kitchen is the soldier's chief information centre, linked as it is daily with the supply lines and the rear. It is something like the village square, from which news is spread abroad. But these rumours were contradictory. Some sent us to Argonne, others to Lorraine, and still others to the Vosges. The optimists were sure that we were going into reserve in the entrenched camp near Paris.

Indeed, we were approaching Paris. Here were Saint-Germain, Saint-Cyr, Versailles, and then Juvisy. Clearly we were going round Paris on the outer circle line.

I do not know at what station, where we did not stop, our assistant medical officer hustled us to the window the better to see the civilians waving at us. A pretty girl shook her handkerchief feverishly. The Major was leaning out of the window of the next compartment, waving his arms and gurgling roguishly, 'Darling, darling!' The medical officer murmured in his working-class voice, 'Eh, there! The Major's going too far. She's my girl, honest. Don't make any mistake about that!'

I lay down on the seat once more. Where were we going? Oh! what did it matter? I had a cowardly feeling of pleasure at letting myself be carried away by fate. I closed my eyes and fell into a beatific sleep to the rhythm of the train. Tomorrow . . . In the army one must live for the present moment and avoid as far as possible thinking of the future, or else one suffers anguish. Happy the ox that does not know it is being led to the slaughter-house.

VII

THE CHAMPAGNE OFFENSIVE
(25TH SEPTEMBER 1915)

AFTER travelling for twenty-four hours we got off the train at Vitry-la-Ville, near Vitry-le-François, in Champagne. The platform had clearly been specially built for troop trains. For thirty-six hours we bivouacked quite near, beside a row of tall poplars. Bivouac: the word used to thrill me long ago when I first read the accounts of the Napoleonic Wars. It had an air of adventure about it. As to adventure, the cold woke me in my tent at 3 o'clock in the morning although it was August. It was enough to put one off camping out for ever.

Then we marched off in a northerly direction, moving by small stages. In order no doubt to avoid both the heat of the day and the curiosity of the German aeroplanes, we set out at sunset. We marched along dry white roads in a cloud of chalk dust between rectangles of black pine-trees, bare hilltops and fields of buckwheat. It was usually my duty to lead the way. I would go ahead, accompanied by a bicyclist, to reconnoitre the crossroads and village turnings, leaving the bicyclist at each point on the route where the column could go astray. Indeed, at night it was very easy to miss one's way in a village, and get lost down a side-road or finish up in a pond. I was sufficiently innocent to be proud of my responsibility and I walked happily along in the moonlight or starlight, whistling *Tipperary*. At about midnight we reached a wood where we bivouacked, or else pitiable billets—a poor village evacuated over a year previously, the walls crumbling, the upholstery and wall-paper damp, a mattress with no sheets, or else just dirty straw. We slept like logs. And after a day spent wandering about getting bored, we set off again for another village.

Finally we had to hold a sector of the front line in the Bois d'Hauzy, on the edge of the Champagne plain and the Argonne forest. This sector was different from the others. No sooner had one dug down eighteen inches in this boggy ground than the water welled up. And then there were no approach trenches to the front line. Instead one reached it through the woods along 'Indian' paths made of duckboards. Instead of proper trenches, wicker baskets filled with earth were supposed to protect the raised gullies which wound along the edge of the wood. Instead of dug-outs we had wooden huts, likewise above ground and at the mercy of every shell. But the quiet was idyllic. The rats were our real enemies. They swarmed everywhere, devouring our bread and rations if we failed to hang them from an iron hook, and sometimes they woke one in the middle of the night by running at full tilt across one's face. Naturally the stench of dead rats was everywhere, and rendered some huts uninhabitable.

We had come to this rather odd sector in order to relieve some units of the Colonial Infantry and African Light Cavalry. The Captain whom we were taking over from was a spare little man with a nose like the blade of a knife, flabby cheeks, and the unsteady look and abrupt movements of an alcoholic. He led us out beyond the front lines, that is to say, into the open fields in front of the wood. In the moonlight I looked nervously towards the dark shape of the Bois de Ville on the farther side of the river Tourbe, which flowed between the two woods, where the enemy was waiting in silence. The Captain caught my glance and hastened to reassure me. The enemy was a long way off, we were covered by the outposts down by the Tourbe and furthermore we were half hidden by the mist, a pungent mist which tasted of soot.

I have never forgotten that walk at night through the silent clearing in the woods, bathed in moonlight and mist, in which I enjoyed at once the poetry of the night and the sharp scent of danger.

Afterwards the Captain invited us to a frugal supper, and, in the absence of forks, we all stabbed with our knives the nearest piece of cold meat on the dish. Then he left us, taking his company with him. We wished him good luck with a certain feeling of respect. As old soldiers and a defence regiment we had a sort of awe of these Colonial troops dedicated to assaults and raids.

'I know perfectly well,' he said, 'that they are only relieving us to make mincemeat of us elsewhere.'

Sure enough, everyone was talking of the forthcoming offensive. Moreover, everything proclaimed it: our own journey, the troop movements around us, the enormous approach trenches dug behind the lines (for the cavalry, it was said), the increase in the number of artillery batteries and ammunition dumps, and the incessant drone of the brown and yellow aeroplanes over our heads, pursued in vain by the enemy shells, whose puffs of white smoke one could see suddenly blossom in the sky like Japanese paper flowers plunged into water, followed afterwards by the muffled explosion. It was at this point that the blue helmets with a flat crest, adorned with a grenade, were issued to us. We tried them on amidst shrieks of laughter, as if they were carnival hats.

We soon had official confirmation of the offensive. While we were being held in reserve in the woods we received a message signed 'J. Joffre' which we were to read to our men. It came from the General Headquarters of the Eastern Armies (General Staff, 3rd Office, No. 8565). It needed exceptional circumstances indeed for this letter to come from such a high level down to us.

Joffre recalled that 'the French soldier fights ever more bravely the better he understands the importance of the actions in which he is engaged, and the more he has confidence in the dispositions made by the High Command'. Officers were therefore requested to inform their men of the favourable conditions of the forthcoming offensive. It was a matter of 'chasing the Germans out of France' in order to liberate our compatriots in the occupied areas, bringing the neutrals in with us (?) and lightening the burden on the Russians.

Joffre added that the offensive would be undertaken by several armies provided with full modern equipment—more than twice as many machine-guns, new field batteries, plentiful supplies of ammunition, motor convoys, and above all heavy artillery. He affirmed that the Germans, fully engaged on the Russian front, 'have only very slender reserves behind the thin line of their entrenchments'. The offensive would be general and would eventually extend to the entire front 'in order to complete the disorganization of the enemy and put him to flight'. It was necessary to 'push without ceasing *both by day and by night* through the second and third lines into open country'.

Open country! What a hope! And to complete our exaltation the note concluded : 'All the cavalry will take part in these attacks in order to exploit the success far in front of the infantry.' The enemy, attacked on all sides, would be unable to concentrate his reserves on one point as he had been able to do at Arras in May 1915 (during the celebrated attack which had made General Pétain's name famous). 'The simultaneousness of the attacks, their strength, their extent . . . are a sure sign of success.'

Was the great General Staff really so sure? In any case, it made us feel so. We firmly believed that the day of glory had arrived, that at last the German lines were going to cave in and that we should set out in pursuit of an enemy in retreat with the aid of the cavalry, held back for nearly a year for 'the break-through'. I let my people know that Paris would soon be able to put out the flags, while at the same time pointing out, in order to lessen their anxiety in advance, that my letters would certainly be delayed. And I told them, arguing with impeccable logic: 'Our chiefs promise us success in such terms that they must be sure of it, for if we were to fail, what a set-back that would be, what a loss in morale for all the fighting men!' I forgot that no one is ever sure of winning. And I did not understand that men can forget better than they can suffer.

The preparatory bombardment, which kept on increasing in strength, filled us with hope. We were in the front line on the banks of the river Tourbe, which could be forded and which we crossed on dangerous planks. We had no trench, but the narrow road down the valley through which the river flowed, was enough to protect us. Our 155s fell regularly with an appalling crash on the edge of the Bois de Ville. From the shelter of a ridge behind us a battery of 75s fired their four guns one after the other, making the air vibrate like four bells striking. The whine of the shells passed over our heads and then, after a brief silence, we heard the four sharp barks as they struck home. Beneath such a deluge of fire we thought that everything in the enemy lines must be reduced to dust.

At last N-day arrived (we did not yet speak of D-day). It was 25th September. Zero-hour was at 09.15 hrs. Alas! it was raining. In selecting this date the General Staff must have forgotten that the equinox nearly always brings with it a south-west wind and rain. This close weather with its low-lying cloud must have considerably hindered our aeroplanes.

Of the attack, in which we played no part since we were on the right pivot and the first not to go over the top, we saw little but black forms advancing slowly in broken lines into the clouds of smoke, in which they soon disappeared.

For a moment it was rumoured that the cavalry had broken through . . . But we soon had to sing a different tune. Despite the number of prisoners and the importance of the positions taken, at the end of a week we had to admit that the offensive had failed, since in front of us there were still new trenches, barbed-wire entanglements, guns, and men. It did not take us long to forget our wild hopes and to get ready for a second winter in the trenches.

VIII

WINTER IN CHAMPAGNE (1915-16)

A TALE OF TWO PRISONERS

We were to spend the entire winter in Champagne.

A bleak land was this barren country of Champagne; almost a desert since even before the war the villages that the news bulletins had made famous—Perthes-lès-Hurlus, Mesnil-lès-Hurlus, Tahure—numbered only a few hundred inhabitants and lay three or four miles apart. I spent All Saints' Day sleeping on the bare earth at an enchanting place marked on the ordnance map 'Hut and Well', a description which said much about the scarcity of dwellings and the shortage of water.

It was depressing to live in this cheerless country of small geometrically regular woods of black pine-trees, and dried-up chalky gullies between bare ridges. Our men from the Vendée, accustomed to a smiling countryside and fertile fields, would remark:

'If those son-of-a-bitch Boches want to keep this bastard country, let 'em have it. It's no bloody loss. It's not worth getting killed for this!'

I refrained from taking the matter up with them and preaching a sermon on national unity, which would have been out of place: I merely smiled. For these 'defeatist' remarks were only

44

said in jest, and at times the men came out with banter of quite another kind. I can still hear one of them, Bréchouard, on his return from Mesnil-lès-Hurlus, which was then undergoing a terrible pounding:

'When I got to Mesnil, they were sending over a packet. You bloody fool, I said to myself, this isn't the time to be here. And there was Joffrion in the middle of eating, and he said, "Look, you bastard, if they want to kill me, they're not going to kill me on an empty belly!"'

When we got into the front line we occupied the old German trenches which had been taken during the offensive of 25th September. The dug-outs had had to be rebuilt, for some of the German ones had been blocked by subsidence, caused by our own bombardment, others served as collective graves for a whole platoon together with its Feld-webel (on one was a notice: 'Twelve German soldiers here'), and most of them, dug as a pro-tection against our 75s and 155s, had their en-trances facing north—that is to say, now facing the German 77s and 105s. Fortunately it was fairly easy to excavate new dug-outs and it was not even necessary to buttress them with wooden props, for the chalk over our heads held of its own accord as if it were blocks of cement. Of course, a heavy shell would have finished them off, but heavy shells were rare in the front line.

I remember a particular dug-out in the second line in which we lived for several weeks. We kept ourselves warm with an improvised stove made of an old milk-can and drain-pipes brought from Perthes-lès-Hurlus. We burnt the stumps of the surrounding pine-trees which had been knocked flat by the bombardment in September. We led the purely physical life of troops in reserve: huge meals served by our orderly, who dressed himself up in a pointed helmet as a joke, heavy wine, fine liqueurs, healthy walks in the dry cold air through the white craters of the old German front line riddled with shells. Admittedly, at the turn of a trench one sometimes saw a blackened and emaciated hand sticking out of the chalk wall, or a boot that was visibly not empty. In another place it would be a German's leg, recognisable by its short boot, which had been cut off clean, half-way up the thigh, and which now lay behind the parapet, withered and apparently mummified by the frost. But we were sufficiently philosophical not to be too affected by these intimations of our possible future. *Hodie mihi, cras tibi,* it is my turn today, it will be yours tomorrow, these dead men should have been saying to us. But we avoided such gloomy thoughts by taking refuge in fatalism: what is written is written.

When men live close together like this for days on end, inevitably incidents occur, especially where officers of different ranks are concerned. We were quartered in the reserve lines with our Commanding Officer, the pallid Major with the brown beard, whom I have already mentioned on the subject of our Colonel. One day, I cannot remember why, he upbraided me bitterly and added:

'It will go down in your report, you know! It'll go down in your report!'

This immediately put my back up:

'My report? But you forget, sir, I'm a reservist. My military career doesn't mean a thing to me! My future lies elsewhere, if I come through. As soon as the war is over I shall return to civilian life—and with pleasure!'

The Major was thrown off his balance by my reply. He had in fact forgotten that I was a reserve officer and had spoken to me as if I were a youth just out of Saint-Cyr, trembling before his Commanding Officer and fearing a bad report which might jeopardize his career and ruin his chances of promotion. It often happens that those in the regular army fail to understand the feelings of reservists.

Our monotonous life was enlivened in November by a comic episode. I was in the Battalion Headquarters in the reserve lines in the Deux-Mamelles sector when a Lieutenant in the front line telephoned from his dug-out that he had taken two prisoners (for we had a telephone in the front line). I myself had lived in that dug-out, a wretched hole dug in the side of a communication trench, with a board to keep the mud from flowing in from the bottom of the trench itself. The only protection against the cold was an old piece of canvas; some straw did for a pillow; but there was the telephone, making a fine contrast between this return to the Cave Age and Modern Science, Progress and all that nonsense.

Well, the front line telephoned the Commanding Officer that two prisoners had been taken. Of course, this had not happened on purpose. Two Germans who had lost their way, had jumped into our lines and had suddenly found themselves face to face with our look-outs, whose fixed bayonets had held them in respect.

In due course the prisoners arrived at Headquarters. The Major had thought it advisable to place his belt on the table with his revolver—

47

though he left it in its holster. Then he ordered the Germans in.

The first was a great big ox of a 2nd Lieutenant who could have been hardly twenty, a young student just out of university, his face pink and beardless, with blue eyes and a large pair of spectacles on his aquiline nose, and a delightful cap with a patent-leather peak and red broadcloth band sitting on his blond head. His tunic was decorated with red piping at the neck. At his side stood a Gefreite, or lance-corporal, small, stocky, with his hair close-shaven, a low forehead and a sly look.

The Major thought he had better warn the prisoners against making any attempt at flight: 'If you try to escape,' he said, pointing to his revolver, 'bang!' The 2nd Lieutenant did not move, but stayed at attention. I was annoyed to feel that dignity was not on our side.

He then told his story in passable French, continually putting on and taking off his leather gloves. Our front line, which had been the German second- or third-line trench, was naturally connected to the new German first line (their former third or fourth line) by old communication trenches choked up with sandbags and *chevaux de frise*—wooden frames covered with barbed wire. As it was night the two men, who were coming up to the front line from the rear, had preferred to walk along the top of the approach trench instead of inside it. In this way they had got lost and had finished up in our lines. 'I haff come to the army,' said the 2nd Lieutenant, 'two veeks ago. I did not know the gutters' [the German *Graben* means both gutter and trench] 'and I expected the Gefreite to guide me.' As to the

48

Gefreite, who was interrogated in German by the battalion sergeant-major, he winked and said, 'Not my fault! the Offizier!' suggesting that he, as a simple soldier, was not responsible, that his job was to follow his officer. We felt that he had known only too well that the Lieutenant was going in the wrong direction, but he had held his tongue in the hope that in this way he would soon be finished with the war.

The Major, no doubt wanting to play the part of an Intelligence Officer, tried to get information about the enemy out of the 2nd Lieutenant, asking him what his regiment was, how long they had been in the front line, and so forth. The German, unmoved and very dignified, replied, 'I cannot speak.' But he added that he was convinced of a German victory and triumphantly threw at us the name Monastir, which the Kaiser's troops had indeed just entered.

Finally the Major rose, signifying that the interview was ended. Thereupon the German said shyly:

'Can I go back now?'

'Go back where?'

'Back to my own lines.'

We all burst out laughing. He was like a child who had been taken 'prisoner' in a game, and was now saying 'Pax' because he wanted to return to his own side.

'But my dear fellow,' said the Major, 'you're mad! What are you thinking of? You've been taken prisoner, you remain a prisoner. Pah! for you the war is finished!'

'But also officer finished. My career is *kaput*. Think. Prisoner after two veeks at ze front!'

Clearly he must have got in the German army's

black books, and he could never have forgiven the French for not having agreed to release him, as if he had been misdealt at a game of cards.

Unless, indeed, he did carve a career out for himself afterwards. Who knows? Perhaps his name was Von Runstedt, Von Manstein or Rommel.

IX

VERDUN

EARLY in May 1916 we were relieved by the 17th Infantry Regiment.

In 1907, the 17th had gained itself a rather unfortunate notoriety. It was at a time when Georges Clemenceau was President of the Council. Encouraged by Marcelin Albert, the vine-growers in the Midi had revolted against the Government. The men of the 17th, sent to Agde and Béziers to re-establish order, had slapped their Colonel in the face, refused to fire on the rebels and mutinied. Our company commander, Captain Quintard, who was a Protestant and therefore leaned politically to the left, said jokingly to me, when we heard that they were relieving us:

'What if we welcome them with the *Song of the Seventeenth* ?'

And he began to hum this song of Montéhus, which is still one of the stock-pieces of the Revolution:

> Salute, salute to you,
> Brave soldiers of the Seventeenth,
> Salute, salute, men true,
> Everyone admires your pluck
> Salute, salute to you,
> To your magnificent deed;
> If you had fired on us
> The Republic would have been shot dead.

But the 17th of 1916 clearly had nothing in

common with the 17th of 1907, and Captain Quintard kept his song to himself when he received the officers who had come to reconnoitre the sector. They had arrived from Verdun, where the battle had been raging since 21st February. The stories they had to tell were not made to reassure us, should our turn come to 'go up' there.

'It's perfectly straightforward. You get relieved when three-quarters of your men have been knocked out. That's the standard rate.'

So my heart froze a few days later when my friend Estève, always imperturbable although he came from the Midi, announced the news as I entered the officers' mess in the village of Juvigny-sur-Marne, where we were resting:

'Young 'un, a great misfortune has overtaken us. The division has been placed under the command of the Second Army. You know what that means? The Second Army is Pétain—and that means Verdun.'

As he spoke he rolled his r's, but he remained perfectly calm and went on reading his newspaper, holding it in his long slender fingers, with his elbows on the mess table. I envied his composure, for my heart was fit to burst. I remembered the remarks the officers of the 17th had made. We were some fifteen officers in the battalion. A dozen of us would be killed or wounded. Would I be one of the three or four who came through?

Suddenly a sharp fanfare of trumpets burst forth on the road and we saw a squadron of cavalry go by, led by their colonel, a thin, gaunt man with a big white moustache. They wore helmets and held tall lances, and stared with disdain from the height of their horses on the untidy infantrymen standing at the farm doors. There were numbers of sergeants looking more elegant than many an infantry officer, with their Sam Brownes and their brown riding boots.

'Hey!' I said to Estève, 'look what fine 2nd Lieutenants that would make us, all that lot!'

'Young 'un,' he replied ironically, 'what are you dreaming about? Most of those fellows have fine families and a fortune and they were marked out for the cavalry. The poor bloody infantry is good enough for us, the Estèves and the Arnauds of this world. . . . And they're holding back all these fellows for the break-through, the famous break-through that we've been waiting for for two years. . . . You know, there's nothing like a lance against machine-guns!'

Opposite us, in front of the shop bearing the sign 'Army Service Stores' which sold the usual range of goods—tins of sardines, pocket mirrors with a sliding wooden cover, tubes of shaving soap, flashlamp batteries, ruled letter paper and yellow envelopes—some of our men were also gazing at the procession. Their faces were set, their looks were stern. Like us they knew that we were going to Verdun—news spread like wildfire among the troops—and like us they were jealous of these 'skrimshankers' who were showing off with their lances. One of them shouted at the last sergeant, a great big boy with a ruddy face, who seemed to be ill at ease:

'It's always the same ones who get killed, isn't it?'

The other pretended not to hear.

At noon the next day we left in lorries.

The men were moving like a herd of sheep towards the crossroads where the convoy of lorries was awaiting us, when Keller, my immediate superior, sprang at me, yelling:

'What's going on here? Why's everyone all over the place? I'll make an example of them!'

Glancing sideways I understood the reason for this sudden outburst of rage. The General, flanked by an over-smart staff officer, was standing by the side of the road, watching our departure. Instinctively the men formed fours and reached the lorries in an orderly fashion. The Lieutenant in command of the convoy was waiting for us, wearing a mixture of uniforms: red trousers, the tunic of a mountain regiment, and a black kepi. He counted the men and entrusted them in groups of twenty to the drivers. 'Just as one would treat cattle sent to the slaughter-house,' I thought bitterly as I climbed into the light lorry reserved for the officers.

We set off in clouds of white dust.

So began our ascent to Verdun, an ascent to Mount Calvary which was to last ten days, ten days in which we had the feeling that we were being carried along on that gigantic supply chain which kept the battle regularly fed, like those bucket-pumps in Mediterranean countries which bring the water up to the parched earth; ten days of piercing agony, which for me were more painful than the nine days that we were to spend in the heart of the battle. The worst mental suffering during wartime occurs when one's thoughts run ahead of one's actions, when the imagination has full rein to contemplate the dangers in advance —and multiplies them a hundredfold. It is well known that the fear of danger is more nerve-wracking than the danger itself, just as the desire is more intoxicating than the fulfilment of it.

Our convoy passed through a suburb of Châlons-sur-Marne. It was 21st May, a Sunday, always an ominous day according to the men of the relief drafts who had seen heavy fighting. The pedestrians watched us go by, some of them with inscrutable or indifferent faces, and this glimpse of the peaceful life in the rear upset us, as happened in the front line when, between bursts of gun-fire, we read what was on at the Paris theatres—*Faust* at the Opéra, *Carmen* at the Opéra-Comique. . . . But other passers-by, particularly the women, looked at us with pity, and sometimes with eyes full of tears. No doubt they had a son, a brother, or their husband at the front.

We travelled for hours in the dust of the dry Champagne countryside, through which the road stretched out between squares and rectangles of black pine-trees, which seemed to be cut out of tin. In the evening we arrived at Belval-en-Argonne, where at last there were ponds and real trees. After dinner, and before going to sleep on the straw at the bottom of a cart in the barnyard, I took a stroll through the village with my brother officers. Towards the north there was a red glow in the sky—probably a barn on fire, 'at Éclaires or Senard,' a peasant told us. I appreciated these old French names, but I saw in this reddish reflection a portent of blood. Farther to the right the sky was dotted with red flashes and greenish-white shell-bursts: an anti-aircraft gun was searching out bomber-planes. And in the peace of the sleeping countryside, one could hear, if one pricked up one's ears, the rumbling of the guns at Verdun.

We remained three days in Belval in boring idleness, which did nothing to improve our morale.

We walked up and down, exchanged rumours, argued steadily. I can still hear the senior medical officer, Truchet, stooping, his legs apart, and a shifty, worried look on his face, scratching his black beard with his left hand more nervously than usual:

'It's wicked! This butchery ought to cease! Why haven't they evacuated Verdun? Thousands of men are massacred in order to hold on to a group of old obsolete forts. It's madness! Oh, what brilliant commanders we have!'

These defeatist remarks, which from a strategical point of view were debatable, received a sharp retort from another officer, the great big Parisian, Menlen, |whose long, thin, bent body swayed backwards and forwards as he held his left hand on his hip:

'You say that, and you a regular? It's you that's wicked. What if the men heard you? It was ideas like that that led to the 15th Corps clearing out in '14!'

He had struck home, for Truchet was from Antibes, the 15th Corps' home ground.

I was to remember this scene with irony later, in July, when this same officer begged and obtained from Truchet immediate evacuation because of heart disease, at the very moment when the regiment received orders to return to Verdun.

Some officers behaved very differently from Truchet. A notable example was Captain Keller. This stocky little man used to walk around the village wearing a plain blue kepi, without any braid, as stiff as a cadet's shako, a cap that he never abandoned, even in the front line, despite the regulations. He claimed that he found a helmet physically unbearable. In actual fact I always suspected that this attitude was pure showmanship: Keller had created for himself a part that made him distinct from other mortals, and this was one of the reasons for his popularity. For he was the hero of the regiment from the day when, in a fit of rather questionable excitement, he made a grenade battle last for two hours when it could have been ended in a couple of minutes. He lost thirty of his men, but he won the Legion of Honour. He owed it to his reputation to react violently to any defeatist remarks, and he did not fail to do so. Someone said to him:

'The latest rumour is that the two regular regiments in the division are to be given front seats at Haudromont. We reservists are going to get a quiet corner on the left bank, either Marre or Charny. The divisional commander told Nivelle that we weren't fit for anything else.'

On hearing these remarks, which probably represented the secret hopes of many of us, Keller went red with anger:

'What's that? The regiment deserves better than that. It can go to Verdun, the same as any other. If necessary I'll go by myself, even if I have to desert in order to fight!'

That evening Estève commented coolly on this outburst of Keller's, 'The word of a toper'. Everyone knew that Keller's loud-mouthed heroism was due as much to drink as to vanity.

We set off again, marching by small stages through the Argonne Forest, beside ponds in which brick-coloured grass dozed on the surface, and through clearings which smelt of freshly cut wood. At one of the ten-minute halts laid down by regulations after fifty minutes' marching, I discovered some territorials with grey moustaches

57

working on a standard gauge railway line which was not marked on my map. I learnt that it was a new line to Fleury-sur-Aire and that it was going to augment the meandering narrow-gauge track which ran from Bar-le-Duc to Verdun and gave the appearance of a child's plaything. One of the territorials, who was old enough to be my father, said, with that critical sense typical of the French soldier:

'They should have built this line long ago!' and added, 'You're going up to Verdun? We were there at the beginning, in February. Four men were killed in our company.'

To this man, who must have been in his forties, it was obvious that the Verdun episode was something out of the ordinary: the territorials were supposed to guard the railway lines in the rear and not go up to the front. But clearly he was not sorry to be able to say that they too had taken part in the battle.

We went on to Vaubécourt and Rembercourt-aux-Pots, both in ruins since 1914. Beside the road we saw the graves of soldiers killed here on 8th September 1914: Private Rémy Bourleux of the 37th regiment of the line; Private Constant Thomas of the 79th regiment of the line. The name and date were painted in white on the cross of black wood. Sometimes, the dead man's faded red kepi was still hanging on the cross. I thought of the battle of nearly two years previous, and of the riflemen in their red trousers beneath the explosions of the shells while the village burnt. To us in helmets and blue uniforms, it seemed to date from another war altogether. But this too spoke to us of death.

Finally we approached the road which 'went

up' from Bar-le-Duc to Verdun, the 'Voie Sacrée', and in the distance we saw the lines of lorries coming from or going to the battle. Sometimes, between the clouds of dust, one could see the sun flashing on their windscreens. We were to be billeted at Erize-la-Grande, beside the road. We reached the first houses of Erize-la-Petite, which is also on the main road, a mile or two south of Erize-la-Grande. A signpost indicated that we were within twenty miles of Verdun. But here we ran into some gendarmes who told us:

'This road is forbidden to columns of infantry, by order of the Army Regulating Commission.'

Thereupon a gaunt little man with no indication of his rank interposed, yelling:

'You'll have to turn back! They should have told you at the previous post and made you go straight through to Erize-la-Grande to avoid the main road.'

As soon as they had piled arms, the men, weary and angry, threw down their packs beside the road amidst oaths and collapsed on the bank. The Colonel trotted up and, disconsolate at the thought that the men would have to undertake a further march of a few miles, tried to arrange matters, but in vain. 'There's nothing to be done—army orders!' shouted the little man, who was full of his sense of duty and delighted to be able to hold out against this fine figure of a Colonel.

But I soon found that we were still in France, the country of string-pulling and getting around regulations. The orderly went to find his commanding officer, who was attached to the Second Army. Fortunately for us, one of our battalions had just received a new commanding officer, a major who had been on the General Staff of the

Army Corps. This major now joined us, introduced himself to the officer of the Second Army, and thus succeeded where the Colonel had failed. Staff officers know how to look after one another. ... As a signal favour the regiment was authorized to march in single file along the side of the road, and thus reach Erize-la-Grande by the direct route instead of having to climb back up the hill.

We remained for two days in this miserable village, where our officers had to sleep four to a room with two beds, ornamented with crucifixes, sprigs of box and mementoes of First Communion —naïve pictures in frames. The houses all stretched out along the road, and were spattered with mud right up to their roofs.

Lorries went past unceasingly, some coming back from Verdun, others going up to the battle. We saw the remnants of the Third Army Corps go by, survivors from the 129th and 36th regiments, their faces as grey as their greatcoats and covered in ten days' beard. Some of them were wearing trophies taken from the Germans—filthy grey helmets or forage-caps. With their legs dangling over the tailboards, they seemed to regard us with hostility, as if to say, 'It's your turn now!' It was said of this Third Army Corps that the men had demonstrated against 'Mangin the Butcher' and had lynched some gendarmes.

More lorries filed past, loaded with spent shell-cases, the copper of which sparkled in the sunlight, and sometimes with the remains of aeroplanes, pale yellow wings with the tricolour markings still fresh. Going up in the other direction were lorries full of recent recruits, with dejected or bantering looks on their faces, and others loaded with long slender 75-mm. shells, fat 220s with brass cases, or thin gas cylinders for the observation balloons. We had already heard of the Army Regulating Commission, which reminded us of the 'regulating stations' which controlled all rail traffic. Indeed, the motor traffic on the Voie Sacrée was as closely timed and regulated as a railway line.

Sometimes a touring-car insinuated itself between the heavy lorries, and one could make out the caps decorated with gold braid or oak leaves and the red, blue or tricolour arm-bands. These were the gentlemen of the General Staff who were masters of our fate, who pushed us about the battlefield like pawns on a chess-board, and for whom we felt at once hatred, scorn and envy. Whenever there was a lull in the procession of lorries we heard the everlasting rumbling of the guns, which had become an obsession for us, like the Trappist's saying, 'Brother, we must die.'

On Sunday 28th May—a Sunday once again —we received a terse order: departure for Moulin-Brûlé by lorry in two hours' time.

As I approached the lorries that were to transport us I met Meulen, who launched into a deep political discussion:

'You know what? They're trying to kill off our men from the Vendée because they are reactionaries and wear a Sacred Heart sown on their greatcoats and a scapular next to their skin. There'll soon be no one left but the radicals from the Midi. What a fine situation that'll be! Yesterday as the 63rd was going by in lorries they threw out leaflets saying "Revolution on 1st June". That's just like the bloody bastards!'

I shrugged my shoulders at the stupidity of these remarks, hoping that our men would not hear

61

them, and climbed into our lorry. The driver had been at the wheel for twenty-four hours. Haggard, exhausted, drowsy, he nibbled a dirty loaf of bread while waiting for us. In 1915 we used to say that 'skrimshanker' was spelt with an A, the A embroidered on the collar of the 'automobilists'. Now we were to discover that though they ran little danger, their lives were not altogether rosy.

We passed through Souilly, the Headquarters of General Nivelle, who had succeeded Pétain. The presence of the General Staff was revealed by the abundance of telephone wires, touring-cars and gendarmes. A little farther on was an airfield with its yellow and green canvas hangars. A small fighter plane about to take off was running along the tarmac, raising two trails of dust. (It was here that I was later to see Georges Carpentier, who was serving in the air corps, practising on a punch-ball.) Farther on again some men were waiting in a field. All had their heads bandaged or their arms in a sling, and they were wearing blue greatcoats. But they carried neither rifle nor equipment, having kept only their gas-mask and their haversack, that all-purpose receptacle stuffed with rations and tobacco, which a soldier gives up only on his death-bed. All of them bore a small piece of red and green cardboard on their chest—their evacuation card. We looked at them with something approaching envy: thanks to their 'cushies' they had for a time ceased to fear.

We got down at Moulin-Brûlé—three wretched houses near where the main Paris–Verdun road crossed the Voie Sacrée. The valley swarmed with green-covered lorries, picketed horses, smoky field-kitchens and men bustling back and forth. This ant-hill in the rear, with its armoured trains, troop

trains, motor transport, cavalry and the baggage of
the units in the line, resembled a painting by Wou-
vermans. Although a heavy German shell would
explode every couple of minutes in the woods on
the right, I was somewhat envious of these
'skrimshankers'—though at the same time despising them—who made war with the minimum of
risk, while the laws of cause and effect had turned
me, a poor little intellectual before the war, into
an infantry lieutenant, that is to say, a man
practically condemned to death barring an unlikely reprieve. And I laughed to think that in
1914 I had been afraid of only one thing: that the
war would be over too quickly, before I had had a
chance to take part.

We climbed the slopes of Bois la Ville, which
was filled with gunners and infantrymen. During
a halt some men from a regiment of the Limousin
who had just come back from the battle, began
to talk to us as old soldiers talk to recruits.

'We had thirty killed in our company. You
don't get relieved till you've lost three-quarters of
your strength, you know that in advance. There
aren't any trenches, just shell-holes which you
link up as best you can. The shells come down
non-stop: you can't even bury your mates. The
worst of all is going up to the front . . .'

Finally I had an instinctive reaction to speak out
violently in order to raise my men's morale and
awaken their *esprit de corps*:

'Get away with you, we've been through it all
already. And a man from the Vendée is worth
any number of Limousins.'

After a night spent in the huts at Bois la Ville,
we set out in the afternoon for the citadel of
Verdun. At the foot of the steep slopes that run

63

down from the Fort of Regret to Thierville Wood we saw a sausage-balloon being brought down for the night by its team at the edge of the trees. I envied these balloonists. . . . Soon the cool dampness of the Meuse reached us. Beyond the river mist one could just make out the dark, silent, dead town of Verdun. We crossed a road at a point where a dull lantern shone on a notice-board: 'Danger Point. Pass Quickly.' A man in a great dark coat watched us cross over from the depths of his sand-bagged shelter. The furtive light from the lamp revealed the emblem of the white grenade on his helmet—a gendarme. I remembered the joke which had gone the rounds of the army: 'The real front begins with the last gendarme.' Was this the last one?

A bridge over a railway line, a road running between mist-laden meadows, zigzagging along-side the river. Suddenly an enormous dark wall, flights of steps, muffled shouts, and the warm odour of cabbage, mouldy bread and creosol. I went down a long vaulted gallery through which passed tip-up trucks drawn by mules, making a deafening din. Doors opened on to typists' offices, engine-rooms and bakeries smelling of warm bread. Then, in the weak electric light, I passed through hall after hall filled with soldiers, some of them changing their clothes after the march for fear of catching a cold—for great danger did not make them forget the little ones— others eating ravenously from their mess-tins and drinking out of their flasks. All these casemates with their tiny windows like portholes and the thick pillars supporting the low ceiling reminded one of the between-decks in a boat full of immi-grants.

I at last reached the room which I was to share with six or seven other officers from the battalion. The only decoration on the whitewashed walls was the inscription: 'Max. weight 600 Kg per sq. metre'—doubtless meant before the war for the quartermasters who must have used this for storing their stocks of biscuit and tins of bully-beef. I thought to myself, 'As cannon fodder we weigh less'. The heat was suffocating. Through the window, which looked on to a gloomy courtyard, there came the filthy stench of soil-tubs. In front the eye was struck by a dark wall which rose like a counterscarp above the well of the courtyard. Shell-bursts, probably from a 380, had made fresh yellow scars on it. One could hear the sound of guns, a heavy metallic boom on three notes, like the bass stops of a cathedral organ: probably a French armoured train firing in the neighbourhood. On the other side the barrage continued as always.

After a summary meal I lay down on my palliasse and tried to work out my chances of survival and of getting out of this fiery furnace unscathed. One out of four would be spared—would I be that one? I drew some comfort from the prediction of that fellow-officer on the train in 1914, who had said that I would 'come through'. I also thought of the little religious medals that my Corsican cousins had sent me, telling me never to be without them 'as they have been blessed by the bishop'. I wore these medals round my neck —despite the fact that a dozen times I had found medals of the Virgin and scapularies on the bodies of men who had been killed. I twitted myself on these superstitions in a free-thinker. Finally, exhaustion overcame me and I slept like a log.

X

THE RELIEF DRAFT

THE following afternoon my heart beat fast as
I read the order that we had just received:
'During the night the 6th battalion will relieve
one battalion of the 301st regiment on Hill 321.
The battalion will leave the citadel at 19.15 hrs.
so as to be at the point where the Bras road meets
the Pied du Gravier gully at 21.00 hrs. Intervals
of fifty yards will be maintained between each
section.' There followed detailed instructions, such
as 'Knapsacks are to be taken but no tools are to
be drawn from stores', which meant that the men
would have with them only their small entrench-
ing tools. I was pleased to see that the other
battalion which made up our regiment was going
to relieve a regular battalion on our right while
we were going to relieve reservists. I naïvely
thought that our sector would be the less fierce.

I stopped short at one of the sentences near the
end: 'The saddle-horses will be in the charge of
2nd Lieutenant Métivier, Special Duties Officer.' I
was filled with rage. He was going to settle down
peacefully in the Sartelles woods while we reserve
officers were going to get killed. He was to look
after the regimental transport including our sabres
—which were only worn on parade—and our
colours—which also appeared only at reviews in
the rear and which were kept rolled up in their
case for fear that they should be taken and earn

special mention in the enemy's news bulletin. How far away were the battles of 1870 with their furious fighting around the regimental colours, scenes which as a child I had so often gazed at on the covers of my exercise books! Now the colours had become skrimshankers and war had lost its panache.

Instinctively I went to see my men. Biscuits, tinned food, cartridges and tools were being distributed among them. The smell of sweat and sour wine flowed through the casemates. As soon as the men caught sight of me they came up and formed a circle around me, and I could just make out their trusting docile looks like dogs in the half darkness. I avoided giving them a patriotic speech which, I felt, would not have gone down well. I restricted myself to repeating and explaining the orders received, and then added:

'Don't worry about this. We've always been a lucky company. We'll come back from Verdun. When you get there, you'll need all the food and cartridges you've got, so take all you're given.'

'That's the worst of it, sir,' one man replied. 'They're trying to load us up like mules, the bloody bastards. We'll never get there!'

'Of course you will. And once you're there you'll be very grateful to have it all with you.'

At moments such as this, it was better to talk to them about practical points rather than their duty.

As the day was drawing to a close we left the citadel and moved through Verdun by sections with a fifty-yard interval between each, in order to reduce losses and prevent panic should a German shell fall plumb on the column. Rue Mazel was in ruins, but it had been cleared for the passage of motor transport and marching columns, the stones being neatly piled on the pavement. A few signboards were still legible: Thibaud, iron-monger; Belrupt, corn merchant. There was a house sliced in two, and on one floor one could see a folding bedstead dangling out into empty space, a cracked mirror in a black frame over a fireplace covered with plaster, and a colour-printed calendar hanging at a slant on a background of faded wall-paper. The silence of the dead town was broken only by the German shells which fell from time to time near the cathedral. We left the ramparts, skirted a public garden, passed on our left the Place de la Gare in which stood a ridiculous statue—doubtless a group dedicated to the memory of the men who fell in 1870 —and reached the Meuse by way of a communication trench dug in the clay behind a line of trees.

The old Galavande bridge was restricted to motor transport. Infantry columns crossed the river on the echoing planks of a pontoon-bridge lower down. As I gazed at the black water flowing through the dark gaps between the pontoons I wondered how many of us would come back over this bridge.

We turned left towards Belleville. During a halt a man with a flabby bloated face and a shifty look came up to me and said:

'I've never been up the line before, sir. I've got a hernia. I was a tailor at the base. Look, sir, here's my certificates.'

Such lack of spunk made me angry and I ordered him in a harsh voice to go off to the company commander. But as I watched him go away, with his head down and his hand clutching his papers, which he hoped would bring him salvation, I said to myself, 'If it weren't for the braid on your arm, wouldn't you try to do the same?' As we set off again we passed a section returning from the battle. The men had a feverish look in their eyes, the flaps of their greatcoats were stiff with dried mud. They were hurrying to the rear, trying to get out as soon as possible from this zone where the shells were still falling. I found myself envying their youthful Lieutenant who was getting away from it all. How I wished I were in his place!

We climbed the slope on the outskirts of Belleville. Through the open windows one could see into the ransacked houses where gunners were bustling about in the light of smoky candles. The bombardment became twice as fierce and the sky over Douaumont on our right glowed luridly. A battery of 75s was firing close by—a dazzling flame followed by a whine, at once brutal and plaintive, which produced reverberating echoes.

Suddenly a flash of light illuminated us, followed by a deafening sharp explosion—it was the first enemy shell. It burst just over our heads, and we instinctively ducked down. We reached the Montgrignon crossroads, but despite its name the village bore no resemblance to one of Jean-Jacques Rousseau's idylls. A gendarme was on duty in a sand-bagged look-out post. This was certainly the last gendarme and the beginning of the real front.

We went one after another along the empty road. We marched and marched through the black night, shattered from time to time by shells bursting on our right. Then we halted, leant against the bank of a damp ditch and waited. What were we waiting for? I remembered the remark of one of the Limousin soldiers: 'The worst of all is moving up to the front,' and I clenched my teeth with fury and wondered, 'What the f.... hell are we doing here?' We set off, only to halt again. A familiar foul acrid stench reached our nostrils—a dead horse left beside the road by the gunners and now putrescent. Finally shadows came towards us—the guides from the regiment we were about to relieve. We set off at a lively pace, across a gully, up steep slopes, over to the right, round to the left. Shells burst on either side. We plunged into a communication trench, climbed out, leapt in again and climbed out once more. I brought up the rear of the last section, marching as if in my sleep. Through my head throbbed the words, 'Knapsacks are to be taken but no tools will be drawn from stores'.

We halted suddenly on a ridge a hundred yards from a danger spot where German 105s were falling with clockwork regularity. I regained the head of the section and asked what was happening. A pitiful voice replied:

'We don't know where the 3rd section has gone. The bastards were running as fast as they could go. We shouted that we couldn't keep up but they took no notice and now we've lost touch.'

Here I was lost in the middle of the night in a sector of which I had not even seen the plan, practically under the fire of 105s, and worried to death by the fact that day was about to break. Something had to be done, so I told the men to follow me and set off in a determined fashion like a shepherd with his sheep, continuing in the direction we had taken up till then. We dropped down into a small valley riddled with shell-holes and full of runnels after the recent rain: 150s burst on the ridge in front in salvoes of four with a thunderous crash, the shell-splinters whistling past our ears like bullets. I halted the men in the shelter of an abandoned communication trench and moved forward to reconnoitre. As always happened, action made me forget the danger.

I reached a wretched dug-out in the side of an embankment, covered with planks to form a roof and with a flap of canvas by way of a door. I tapped on the canvas, as if I could be heard through the din of the bombardment. No answer. I lifted the canvas flap. Two officers were sitting dozing with a candle between them. I asked them if they knew where Hill 321 was. One of them answered in a weary voice:

'No, we don't even know where we are on the map. I've come to replace the battalion commander who was killed here. Besides, this part is dangerous and you'd do well to move on.'

I took his advice and left. Later I was to learn that these two officers had been killed shortly afterwards. . . . Instinctively I went off to the right. I could already feel the cold stir in the air announcing dawn. I hurried on, followed by swinging bayonets and canteens. As long as we arrived before daybreak! In the distance the outline of the ridge began to appear against the still dark sky. The bombardment became fiercer, as it always did before dawn. 'Keep on! Keep on!'

Dug-outs and figures at last—the Battalion Commander. I explained the situation to him in a couple of words and seized on a corporal from the company that I was supposed to be relieving, and before he could recover himself I had pushed him in front of me to act as guide. We climbed an interminably steep slope. A vague grey light

71

slowly revealed the path we were following in the semi-darkness. 'Keep going, keep going!' We reached the top and ran across a ridge with shells bursting almost between our legs. At last I recognized the silhouette of the Captain against the whitening sky.

'There you are! Quick, the enemy is over there,' and he pointed. 'Here's the trench. Make yourselves at home down there. It's the front line. Good night.' And he disappeared.

The section hurriedly crouched down in the trench, which was merely a ditch less than three feet deep. The men huddled together one against the other. Exhausted with fatigue I sank down in a stunned condition. I curled up with my head between my knees and thought, 'The worst of all is moving up to the front.' We had survived this time. It was so good no longer having to march, to run, to move. . . . I was on the battlefield of Verdun but was hardly conscious of the fact.

XI

IN THE LINE

OUR trench lay on a ridge, at a point where the land fell away to the north and east. On the slopes on both sides one could see bare tree-trunks, the branches lopped off by shells. These were the remains of Nawé Wood. To the north lay the enemy, invisible as usual. Beyond the gully, the Ravine de la Dame, which of course we could not see, was a succession of hills. One, higher and steeper than the rest, was still green after three months of fighting. This was what remained of Haudromont and Chaufour Woods, made famous by the news bulletins of March. Brown silhouettes —the Boches—walked calmly up and down this hill, and I felt furious with our artillery for not making them take shelter.

To the left the view was limited by the plateau on which we were entrenched. On the right, beyond the entrance to the Ravine de la Dame, was a pile of white rubble—all that remained of Thiaumont Farm. In front of this zigzagged the French and German trenches, the French line being held by our own 5th battalion. Dominating the whole area, like Vesuvius overlooking the Bay of Naples, was Fort Douaumont, which had been taken by the Germans and which the French bombarded unceasingly. It was continuously enveloped in greyish smoke, punctuated from time to time by black shell-bursts. Finally, behind us, beyond the valley at the end of the Ravine de la Dame which formed a semi-circle of low ground around us, rose the hill of Froideterre with the Thiaumont redoubt on its summit. There the German 305s burst at regular intervals, falling with a cat-like miaouw and raising geysers of brown earth. As at Douaumont, there was not a tree, not a blade of grass. The earth was brown and riddled with craters, like a picture of the moon.

Such was the country around us. But I forgot: a few yards behind us lay a corpse, its head wrapped in canvas, its blue greatcoat turning to grey. It was one of the dead from the previous regiment and there had not been time to cover it with earth. Such a sight was too familiar to affect us.

The gun-fire was kept up without respite. Out of curiosity I counted the number of explosions per minute: about sixty. Thank God, as long as the 150s fell to the left and the 105s to our rear we were spared for the moment. The French artillery seemed to retort feebly in our sector, except for a battery of 155s which fired shells in salvoes of four into the Ravine de la Dame in front of us. Each shell sounded like a cart clattering down a steep slope with the brake jammed on hard, the noise decreasing until the final muffled explosion. Moreover, one felt that the artillery on either side was firing blind into the mass.

German aeroplanes appeared over the German lines, their engines humming and throbbing like singing-tops. Behind us two of our biplanes, Farman 'hen-coops', circled apprehensively, hesitating and then turning prudently to the rear when a Fokker came and threatened them. Like a properly embittered infantryman I thought, 'So that's our mastery of the air!'

So the hours passed. From time to time one had to crawl behind the trench in order to satisfy a call of nature—a subject never mentioned in war novels. There one risked an ignominious end (how many soldiers have been killed while they were in 'the bushes'—a euphemism used to describe a place far from poetic!), an accident which a mention in dispatches would happily transform into a glorious death.

Sometimes the word went round, 'Martin has been wounded. . . . Bérard has been killed by a machine-gun bullet.' Towards evening the bombardment increased, and it seemed to me that the 150s which were falling on our left flank, were getting closer. I thought of the heavy gun on the side of a gulley in front, camouflaged in blue and green, methodically served by blond giants in field-grey, their brows streaming with sweat, passing the shells from hand to hand, loading and firing with the regularity of a team from Krupps. If the ground were a bit softer under the left wheel than under the right, the gun would sink a little to one side, and that would be enough eventually for the shells to reach us. . . .

Suddenly we heard a strange sound, a gasping whine, which sharply descended the scale to end in a muffled explosion a few yards in front of our trench. It was a French battery of an unusual calibre, 90 mm. or 120 mm., firing on us. Livid more with rage than fear, I seized the Very pistol and fired the alarm signal into the air—six green stars which fell back to earth in a cluster. As if to be ironic, the gunners replied with a group of shells which dropped behind our trench. We were being straddled by our own guns. Fortunately, all these shells appeared to have poor fuses and burst in the earth without doing much harm. I was no less furious for that. I made scarcely any distinction between French and German artillery, since I seemed to be their common target.

After dark the bombardment around us calmed down a little. Shadows came out of their holes. Men collected the canteens of their mates and went off to get their rations. They knew where to find the field-kitchens in the gully of the Pied de Gravier through the same mysterious grape-vine that kept them informed of all the latest news, whether it concerned Captain Eckard's escapades in Paris, the Brigadier's imminent removal from his command or the next draft of reliefs. In this unknown land in the midst of shell-holes they instinctively found their way, arrived at the field-kitchen and took their rations of meat, vegetables and bread. In the light of a smoky candle one of the cooks filled their flasks with two mugs each of wine—wine as precious as bread—with the care of a milkmaid measuring out her milk. Then, carrying the canteens full of soup and meat, the flasks slung over their shoulders like bandoliers, their haversacks stuffed with bread, and holding a bag containing letters and parcels, they would return in the dark under the everlasting whirr of the 105s, and, all being well, would rejoin us before break of day.

In the same way my batman managed to discover a spring at the bottom of a gully in our rear, from which he brought back buckets of cool water which were a delight after a day of burning sun, dust and smoke.

Around midnight I would visit the company commander, whose command post was a shelter in the side of a communication trench, under a lopped twisted tree, some twenty yards behind my trench. I found him as always wearing his blue kepi. He was very restless, giving orders here and there, having his communication trench re-dug, sending up a working party to the officer in command of the section on the right, for on that flank the enemy were closer and also more aggressive, continually sending over grenades or incendiary bombs which did little damage but kept our men in an unnerving state of tension. From my section I hardly noticed them. Distances seem long between men in trenches.

While I was with the company commander an orderly arrived from the battalion command post bearing a note, and this worried me. Were they going to ask our men to attack, men who were only suited for defence and who had had no assault training? But the message merely warned us of a German attack to be launched in the morning: 'Lieutenant Gaillard, of the 5th Battalion, has reported increased activity in the enemy lines; in particular he has seen the enemy place a machine-gun in position.' I was relieved. This news was no surprise to us. Every morning one was bound to expect an enemy offensive. At that moment the officers' dinner arrived from the Radet Barracks at Verdun, and I ate with delight a quarter of young wild boar which our cook had succeeded in marinading for several days. Out of my mug tasting of iron I drank the heavy commissariat wine, which eventually stained both mugs and flasks a dark violet. I returned to my shelter in a more cheerful mood—for morale is fortified by physical satisfaction. I persuaded my men to dig themselves farther in against the enfilading fire of the German machine-guns at Thiaumont Farm, and then I slept like a log, indifferent to the gun-fire, the coldness of the June night and the threats of the coming dawn.

The days passed monotonously to the sound of gun-fire, which one eventually ceased to hear, as one ceases to notice the roar of the waves at the sea-side. The only events were the scraps of news passed from man to man: so-and-so was dead, so-and-so wounded. I realized later that Ascension Day had come and gone. We had already lost count of time.

One night I had to show a working party of young soldiers from the 125th to their positions. They had been sent to us 'to dig a support trench behind our front line'. I had a fit of anger when I received this order. The position of this second line was merely a string of shell-holes made by 150s, for it was a familiar target for the German artillery. And furthermore, what was the point of a support line when we had no troops to man it? But this theoretical application of the rules of war was clearly one of the General Staff's ideas. The Regiment had to be able to send to the Division, the Division to the Army Corps, the Army Corps to the Army, the Army to the Army Group, the Army Group to General Headquarters, a lovely report with a plan of the sector showing the double line of trenches in blue and the machine-gun emplacements in green. . . .

Of course I said nothing of this to the officer cadet who brought up the 125th's working party. I showed the direction in which the trench should be dug, my only reference point being the moon. . . . These young soldiers were pretty nervous, as one always is in a new sector where one does not yet know the dangers. They cast worried glances to the left, where 77s were bursting every thirty seconds, only a hundred yards away. I reassured them, and got a certain amount of conceited pleasure out of my protective attitude to these raw recruits.

'You've got nothing to worry about,' I said. 'The Boches only shell this part during the daytime. At night they only send over 77s, which are just snowballs, and then they always fall on the left flank. There's not a soul there, but that makes no difference. You know, there's no bigger fool than a gunner. Once he's begun firing somewhere he sees no reason to stop.'

When I had got back to my trench I saw an unforgettable sight. Our bombers must have been making a raid behind the enemy lines. All along the enemy front searchlights were springing to life. One could see their long yellow pencils scanning the night sky and sweeping back and forth with astonishing rapidity. Some were lost in the dark sky, others were blocked by the low cloud. I thought of the German alert, of the searchlight lorries coming out of their hiding-places made of branches and raffia and suddenly blazing forth into the black night, the anti-aircraft guns, their muzzles pointing to the stars, the gun-crews standing at attention, and in the high-ceilinged rooms of the ransacked châteaux German staff officers on the telephone. I did not have the feeling that our own organization was as perfect. Luckily, we might be saved by the very nature of our shortcomings—our individuality. 'To shift for oneself' is not a phrase that can be translated into German.

That same night I watched a group of casualties

from our right flank moving to the rear. A French 155 had killed five men and wounded seven. One of them was writhing with pain on his stretcher, his head smothered in bandages which formed a blob of white in the darkness. I had another fit of anger over these 'mistakes', this senseless muddle. My only consolation was that the enemy was in the same boat. Though it was in vain that we sent up our green Very lights in order to implore our gunners to lengthen their range, the pink Very lights of the enemy in front seemed to be equally ineffectual.

The following morning we learnt that a heavy German shell, possibly a 420, had broken through the concrete redoubt at Thiaumont, the command post of the Colonel of the 293rd, which, with our own regiment, formed our brigade, and had blown up a supply dump of grenades and flares. The Colonel had been wounded, his sappers and telephonists wounded or killed. Our front-line troops had no sympathy for these 'skrim-shankers'.

On the same day a runner tumbled into my trench out of breath, having just passed through a barrage of 105s. He brought an urgent message which I sent on to the company commander, who immediately sent it back to me. We were being asked for a return of officers equipped with prism binoculars. I swore inwardly at such criminal stupidity, which risked men's lives for the sake of red tape. But I was careful to say nothing to my men.

XII

THE ARTILLERY POUNDING

O_{NE} day—I realized later it was a Sunday—
a dozen Fokkers flew over our sector. The
day after, salvoes of 77s suddenly skimmed over
our trench and made us all keep our heads down.
More than that I took no notice. In a calm sector
the arrival of an enemy aeroplane or of a few
shells worried us and made us fear an assault or
a surprise attack. Here, in the heart of the battle,
I remained oblivious to the evidence, however
obvious, that the enemy was observing our lines.
My little niche between two heaps of sand-bags
had become so familiar to me and I felt so at
home in it that I could not conceive of the Germans getting me there.

On the same day it was announced that one of
our aeroplanes was also going to observe our lines:
we were to place Bengal lights on the edge of the
trenches and set them off at a signal from the
aeroplane—a six-star flare. But our Breguet made
only a timid appearance in the rear and did not
dare to fly above us—held in check, no doubt, by
the Fokkers. 'Our mastery of the air again,' I
muttered bitterly.

In the evening a large splinter from a 210 which
had burst on the remains of the Thiaumont redoubt, 800 yards in our rear, flew through the air
with a horrible swishing sound and hit one of our
men, Soulard, in the shoulder. He immediately

81

walked off to the rear, his arm in a sling under the empty sleeve of his tunic, feverish, anxious to get out of this hell, and envied by his mates—who were most surprised to learn later that his wound had proved fatal.

As night fell a storm broke. The peals of thunder were more magnificent than the gun-fire and shell-bursts of even our largest guns. As if humiliated the batteries on both sides remained silent. Those who were religious probably thought that they were listening to the voice of God hurling anathema on mankind for such self-slaughter. I was simply aware of the pettiness and feebleness of man confronted with the power and everlastingness of nature, as I had been in my childhood before the immensity of the sea and the perpetual onrush of the waves. But at the same time I felt in communion with the universe, and this vague pantheism comforted me.

The next day the men passed along a message which the Captain had sent on to me. It was a bombastic order signed by General Nivelle, in which I read amongst other things: 'The storm is gathering along the British front, it is gathering along the Russian front. . . . Stand firm, men!' I was about to shrug my shoulders, but restrained myself as the men were watching me. I refrained from reading out the text and limited myself to announcing the allied offensives. I knew better than the staff-officers what one could say to the men and particularly what one could not say. I could imagine what their reactions would have been to that pompous message:

'The old bastard has only to come down here with his arse-lickers if he wants to stand firm! He'll find out what it's like far better than in his town hall at Souilly. If the son of a bitch sent some of his frigging staff-officers down here they wouldn't put so many fellows into the front line just to get 'em blasted to hell quicker.'

On 6th June the pounding of our trench commenced. Judging by the shell-bursts I imagined that our sector was being swept by two batteries of four 150s each—slow, heavy, solid guns developed at leisure before the war, more Germanic perhaps than other calibres. They were not like the 210s with their muffled rumble, which continued to raise geysers of brown earth in the rear, around the Thiaumont redoubt. Nor were they like the Austrian 130s, which fired with wondrous rapidity and burst into great greenish blooms above the gullies as if at the command of a sorcerer's wand, before the dull racking explosion reached one's ears. These 150s, with their innocent rumble like a cart with the break on, raised columns of earth, stone and broken branches at regular intervals.

I crouched down under the purely moral protection of the knapsack which I always took with me on days of heavy fighting. From time to time, between salvoes, I glanced over the ground in front to make sure that the enemy was not making an assault under its own fire-screen, as had happened in the past. Before huddling down again I would raise my eyes and watch the four shells pass over the trench in a parabola—four thin black bottles rumbling across the grey sky to explode, after a very short silence, just behind our trench—for the enemy's range was fortunately a little too long.

This gun-fire was kept up, monotonously, for hours on end. In a calm sector a single shell would unnerve me, I had the feeling that my heart had stopped dead, only to begin thumping in my chest afterwards. Here the bombardment had become so familiar that we hardly noticed it any more—as long as the range was too long. At the same time I thought that the guns must surely recoil slightly at each shot, that the range would shorten bit by bit, and that then . . .

What then? There was, of course, no question of running away. Even if military regulations and plain common decency had not forbidden it, it would have taken extraordinary courage to climb out over the top and expose oneself to the shell-bursts and machine-gun fire instead of lying huddled at the bottom of the trench where chance had led us. We were told to stand firm: was there so much merit in staying where one was in the trench where one was pinned down and waiting passively for the end of the artillery pounding when one was physically incapable of doing anything else?

I exercised patience, of necessity. But I was not resigned to the worst. I could not imagine a shell falling plumb on top of our bit of the trench, the impact, the whip-lash of burning metal tearing the flesh, the screams of the wounded and the sudden death or the slow agony . . . Though death brushed me by every minute, I felt within me the will to live, the certainty of survival. They say that those who are going to be killed have a foreboding, that their desire to live has left them. I on the other hand had faith in my luck, while still suffering the physical agony of the hunted animal.

Not all shells kill—in fact, very few of them do. But so many of them were falling this time that some of them struck home. The ominous news was passed from mouth to mouth down this frail string of men crouched at the bottom of their narrow ditch: 'Sergeant-Major Genais has been killed . . . Sergeant Boutaud has been wounded in the stomach . . . Two have had it in the 4th section . . . The two machine-gunners on the left have been buried . . .' In each case I imagined the man concerned and attributed to him a melancholy look, as if he had known that he was doomed.

The bad news increased. Though the small group of men, who were so close that I could signal to them by hand, had so far been spared, the losses around us were heavy. Sergeant Aynac of the 1st section, killed; Bonhoure, the runner who loved his drop of wine when resting, killed; Mafieu, the ex-cook who had been sent up the line again as a punishment for getting drunk one night, killed; the three machine-gunners near the Captain, killed. . . . Finally, it became too much. The sight of these bundles of weak flesh waiting for death under a hail of steel and fire revolted me. At that moment I only thought of Providence in order to deny it or curse it. Morand, my orderly, had said in his simple way: 'How can God allow such things? He can't be thinking of us now!' Heaven, indeed, was empty. There was no concept of sin which could give sense to such massacre.

I came to realize later that this revolt against martyrdom, this sense of pity for innocent victims, was a sign of my deep yearning for justice—the spiritual flame at the centre of my mortal being.

The bombardment, which had slackened during the night, returned the next day with renewed fury. I ended up almost unaware of the danger, and though I lowered my head when a 150 fell near, it was purely a reflex action and my heart no longer beat faster than usual. I heard without emotion that Loizeau had been killed, that Corporal Butard had lost an arm, that Belleu had received a head wound. This state of indifference is perhaps the best thing for a man in the heart of the battle: to act by habit and by instinct, without hope and without fear. . . . This long run of excessive emotion had finished by killing in me emotion itself.

XIII

THE GERMAN ATTACK

THE sun was already high in the sky and it was
warm when the pounding ceased around us,
though continuing even more fiercely in our rear.
There was a minute of calm and, as it were, of
meditation. Was this the attack at last, the attack
that I no longer wished to believe in? As a precaution I passed along the order to inspect rifles,
to see that they were loaded and to clean the
ends of the barrels, which are inclined to become
blocked up with earth after hours of bombardment. And then I looked towards the enemy lines.

The landscape was now familiar to me. In the
foreground were the remains of our network of
coiled wire, twisted and tangled like enormous
broken spiral springs, then a few trunks of pine-
trees mowed down by the shells almost to ground
level, and finally the counterslope running down
to the Ravine de la Dame where the enemy were
hidden. Suddenly my eye was caught by two dark
shapes like garden cloches on the ground fifty
yards away—two helmets, two Germans doubtless
ready to leap forward. I hurriedly sent word to
warn the Captain. One of the Germans waved
his arm: was it a sign of friendship intended to
invite us to 'be friends'? Or was it not rather a
signal? In fact, a few seconds later I saw grey
forms begin to move in front of us and the shooting burst out crackling on all sides. It was only

later that I discovered that two of the machine-guns near us had opened fire on the enemy waves across the Ravine de la Dame, who were going into the assault on our right, and that from their side the German machine-guns were firing at us.

'Shoot low!' I shouted at my men, 'for God's sake, shoot low!' One man near me, Bouron, white with funk, had huddled up so as not to show his head above the trench: he must have been firing at the sky. I shouted at him to shoot low. He cast the look of a hunted animal at me, stealthily raised his head and fired right ahead of him with his eyes shut. I shrugged my shoulders, took a rifle and began to fire myself. The racket of the shots and the smell like garlic of the powder quickly went to my head: 'Shoot the bastards, shoot!' I suddenly noticed a large fellow across my right, I aimed, I had the feeling of the marks-man who has got his target, I pressed on the trigger and while I took the recoil on my shoulder the fellow disappeared. I wondered later whether it was my bullet or someone else's that had hit him, or whether he had simply thrown himself to the ground because he found the rifle-fire too much. In any case, he was the only German I believed I hit in three and a half years of fighting, and even then I was not sure.

Suddenly there was nothing to see: all the Boches had disappeared. What had happened? 'But the bastards are shooting,' I said. 'Fire! Fire!' Beside me on my left Vidal, good old Sergeant Vidal, with his black beard and the sad look in his eye, reeled and lowered his head. In a blurred way, and without stopping firing, I thought: 'Vidal is wounded, he must have got a bullet in his shoulder.' Vidal pulled himself together, reloaded and raised his head to fire again. He fell to the ground: a bullet had hit him right in the forehead. I guessed rather than saw what had happened. I went on firing away furiously when a heavy blow on my head stunned me. 'I'm wounded,' I said, letting go of my rifle. I slid into a sitting position on the fire-step, with my back to the enemy. I took off my helmet and felt the top of my head. My hair was burning. I passed my fingers through it and held them in front of my eyes to see the blood—and I saw nothing. Then I discovered that my helmet had lost its crest. A bullet fired by one of the Germans lying thirty or forty yards in front had knocked off the crest and brushed through my hair. I was not greatly affected by this, but turning to Morand I said, 'I have just had a lucky escape! The bloody swine!'

But Augereau, the skinny sergeant with the ferrety eyes and pointed chin, who was on the right, suddenly cried out. 'My God, bring up some hand grenades! They're setting up a machine-gun in front of us!' I pulled myself together and organized a chain of men to pass along the grenades, fat lemons of black steel with grooves running up and down and across, forming little squares which broke into fragments when they exploded. All of a sudden a man uttered a terrible cry and collapsed six feet away. It was Mallard, a man from the Vendée, with square shoulders, black hair and a child's blue eyes. With my mouth clenched tight I leant over to discover what had happened. The igniter, which was implanted in the body of the grenade and stuck out at the end, was protected by only a poor cardboard casing. A grenade must have fallen to the bottom of the trench, the shock had primed it and it had exploded in Mallard's legs. I wanted to dress his wounds but it was essential to go on handing up the grenades to Augereau, who continued to throw them with all his strength, swaying on his hips and moving his arm in great semi-circles over the trench. At last he grew tired and gave up.

Mallard was whimpering and saliva was trickling down his lips as he asked me to take off his boot, and the sentence finished in a moan. I leant over him. His foot had been cut nearly clean off by the explosion and only a few shreds of red flesh still joined it to the leg. Underneath, the ground was saturated with blood and a brown stain was growing larger and larger. I removed the remains of the boot from the foot. 'There you are, old chap,' I said. 'No, take off my boot, I can feel it, it's hanging down!' 'You poor fellow,' I thought, 'it's your foot that's hanging down!' Morand and I did the best we could to stop the flow of blood with bandages, but Mallard had already lost a great deal, and it was perhaps too late.

I had not the least feeling of anger for the half-wits or the criminals who had signed contracts for the supply of grenades with cardboard igniter casings and who had once again killed one of our men. It was just one of the risks one ran. Nor did I make any distinction between Vidal, wounded in the shoulder and then killed when he got up again to carry on shooting, and Mallard, the inglorious victim of clumsiness as well as criminal malpractice.

Between the body of Vidal stretched out at the bottom of the trench, and Mallard who continued

90

to implore someone to take off his boot, I was selfishly enjoying a moment's relaxation when the Captain sent for me. I reached him along a poor communication trench which our reserve section had begun. I found him with a vacant expression on his face and the corner of his mouth strangely twisted. He had clearly being doping himself with tots of brandy. He made me drink half a mug of the stuff and then said:

'Combes (the officer in command of the section on the right) has had it. He's got a bullet in the kidneys. You'll have to take over from him for I've absolutely got to have an officer on that flank, it's the danger point of the whole sector. But be careful. Combes was wounded by that bloody machine-gun which enfilades the whole trench from the top of the Ravine de la Dame. So don't do anything rash. I've only got you, so don't go and get yourself shot to pieces. There can't be many left over there. If you need more men I'll send you some from the reserve section.'

'Right,' I said simply. This dangerous new position and poor Combes's wound left me equally unmoved. I joined Combes, who lay at the bottom of the trench, his eyes dim, his face grey. A little saliva flowed from the corners of his mouth down his square chin.

'Well, old chap, you're not feeling too good?' I asked, taking hold of his hand.

'I'm paralysed,' he replied in a low voice without a note of complaint, as if he were indifferent to it all. He had been hit in the vertebral column and not in the kidneys.

'Nonsense,' I said, trying to be reassuring, 'they'll patch that all up at the dressing-station.'

Combes closed his eyes, as if to show that he

knew it would not be . . . He could no longer move his head . . . He died at the dressing-station the following day.

As I was moving forward to study the lie of the land one of the men, Ollivier, a small fellow with straight, blond hair and a sharp, honest look, stopped me, saying, 'Be careful, sir. The machine-gun is still firing. That was what wounded Lieutenant Combes. Look!' And he pointed to a row of little flecks of dust which suddenly sprang up at regular intervals along the wall of the trench on our right.

'And who have we got on our right?' I asked. 'I don't think there is anyone left there,' he replied. I carefully raised my head in the shelter of a traverse. A few yards away stood a Hotchkiss machine-gun. To the right lay the body of the gunner, to the left lay that of the loader. Farther beyond, the trench suddenly dipped down to the bottom of the Ravine de la Dame and there there were only bodies. The German machine-gun had spared no one. As a poor compensation, quite near us we could see the body of a German who had become detached from the assault wave and who had miraculously got that far before being killed by a revolver bullet.

Something had to be done. I asked the Captain for a work party and had a wall of sand-bags put up in order to command the outlet of the un-manned trench. I became completely involved in the job and no longer thought of the danger. There was nothing meritorious about this, I was merely playing my part as an officer. But I would have had no excuse if I had been paralysed with fear.

Ollivier suddenly stopped piling earth into the

sand-bags and bouncing them up and down on the trench floor. He pricked up one ear. 'Someone's coming up in that direction,' he said. In fact an orderly from the company on our right was making his way between the still warm corpses and soon reached us safe and sound. He was looking for the battalion bomber section. He told me that Captain Ancelin had been killed. I well remember that worthy country solicitor, so unwarlike despite the military bearing which he affected, I remember his stocky figure, his legs a little knock-kneed, his everlasting red leather gloves. . . . He had been wounded in Champagne in September 1915 and could therefore consider that he had had his share.

'While waiting for the battalion bombers,' the orderly went on, 'there is a request, sir, to send down one or two cases of grenades.' I turned to a man with a blotchy face and shifty eyes, called Montagne, who was standing by. Montagne jibbed at the idea. 'What about waiting till it's dark?' he suggested. 'But they're asking for these grenades immediately,' I replied. 'Immediately's easy to say . . .' he muttered. I could control myself no longer. 'All right, then,' I said, 'if you funk it I'll go myself.' I had already lifted up the two cases of grenades when Ollivier intervened. 'No, no, sir, you can't do that. I'll go myself and don't worry, I'll come back.' He set off and I watched him go. I was worried, and regretted not having pushed my revolver in Montagne's face. It was a great relief to me when he returned twenty minutes later. 'Well done, Ollivier,' I said, 'well done!' He blushed at the compliment. He had given me back my faith in mankind.

A little later the bomber section arrived, led

by Lieutenant Richard, with his anxious eyes and nervous gestures. I recognized my old corporal, Jaud, amongst them, dark and tanned still, with his soft moist baby's eyes in a face surrounded by a horrible beard. I warned them to take care. Jaud crawled out first, holding a sackful of grenades in his left hand. Richard followed him. Suddenly there was a terrible explosion. Richard reappeared, his face haggard, gasping for air in the midst of a thick cloud of yellowish smoke. Was it an attack? 'To your posts!' I shouted. But I soon understood what had happened. While pulling his sack of grenades after him Jaud must have knocked one of the igniters which were so badly protected by the cardboard casing, and the whole lot had gone up. I put my head forward carefully and saw two bodies. Jaud had a leg smashed and his fore-arm cut to bits. His face was black from the powder. Beside him Ollivier, who had been on guard by the wall of sand-bags, had fallen to the ground without letting go of his rifle. I was deeply distressed over both of them. Jaud had once shown me a photograph of his mother and his wife, robust women from the Vendée who at that very moment should have been knitting in the farmhouse and thinking of their absent one. Ollivier had just shown great gallantry and in return had been struck down by blind fate, while Montagne had escaped. 'A fine example of immanent injustice,' I thought bitterly.

Nevertheless, the bomber section set out again, led by Sergeant Cartelier, a former cook who proved himself a good soldier. He was a great tall, thin, gaunt man with a hatchet face, who wore small, short boots of hardly regulation pattern. I renewed my warning to take care.

'It's all right,' he answered, 'the runner's just got through safely.'

They crawled out, brushing past Jaud's scorched and shattered body. I watched them go, anxiously. They had got half-way up when the machine-gun began to fire savagely. They had been spotted. I imagined rather than saw the men crawling desperately in search of a crevice where they could crouch down out of the way of that hail of fire. But Cartelier, recognizable from his small boots, lay full length on his stomach in the communication trench. He had been caught on the spot by the first burst of gun-fire.

Although death had by now become familiar to us, I felt a sense of disgust when faced with such an appalling waste of human lives, a sense of revolt against the folly of war. . . .

XIV

AFTER THE ATTACK

LITTLE by little the bombardment increased again. It had never ceased completely and from time to time shells had fallen behind us. The German gunners had been overshooting on purpose while awaiting the outcome of the attack. But by midday they must have been informed of the infantry's failure, for they resumed the regular pounding of our line.

The continual bombardment had no effect on me. I watched with indifference the black bottles pass over our heads and explode a short distance in our rear. Some burst in front of our trench, others fell directly on to our line on the left. I did not even bother to raise my arm to protect myself against the pebbles and twigs which were thrown up in a fountain by each shell, and then fell down like rain.

I realized that Morand, my faithful orderly, had not followed me to my new post but had remained in the sector on our left where the 150s were falling thick and fast, and this upset me. I had a strange superstition that his fate was some-how linked with mine. It seemed to me that this big red-faced lad had not been marked down to die and that we should live through every danger together. Why had I not told him to come with me? I was worried that he was separated from me.

But there was work to be done. A new German attack could be expected. I saw that a row of uncapped grenades was placed along the top of the parapet, I loaded a rifle, I posted my few men at a distance from one another, and I waited.

We would stand fast as best we could. If we were outnumbered we would try to withdraw to the protection of the counterslope in the ravine, even if we received a bullet in our backs. Anything rather than be taken.

Night fell without any further assault. The Germans had definitely been discouraged by our resistance. I went to see the Captain, whom I found very depressed: brandy had failed to sustain him any more. 'It's horrible,' he said. 'On the left they're all dead, every one of them!' My heart sank when I thought of Morand. At that very moment a familiar figure appeared before me and said cheerily, 'Well, sir, what have the bastards done to us!' I shook his hand in a sudden outburst of joy. So it was written that he and I should both come through.

We received the reinforcements that the Captain had requested in the morning—a section of Bretons from the 410th and a section of Limousins from the 125th. I had hardly had time to show them their posts when a sentry sounded the alarm. Rifle-fire broke out. I saw a corporal from the 410th peel off his tunic in a moment and start throwing grenades with the regularity of clockwork. He calmly primed each grenade by knocking it on a flat stone on the edge of the parapet and, like a discus-thrower, swung it sizzling into the night where it shortly burst with a violent sharp explosion.

Was it a false alarm? The sentry was sure that

97

he had seen shadows moving in front of him. Perhaps they were German stretcher-bearers come to collect their wounded. But we were no longer in the days of truces between battles. And often, or so we had been told, enemy soldiers would approach under cover of the Red Cross, concealing a machine-gun in their stretcher.

After a period of quiet, another alarm. At that very moment a small man from the company on our flank, the 21st, came up on my left, carrying a case of grenades back to his company. 'Well, we might just as well chuck some from here,' he said merrily in the darkness. 'That'll at least make less for me to carry!' He had already thrown four or five when a yellow flash dazzled me, followed by an explosion so deafening that I thought it had burst my left ear-drum. 'I'm hurt!' I yelled. Somebody said, 'Careful, sir, the Boches will hear you!' On my left the little man from the 21st lay crumpled in a heap. I leaned over his body and realized that his presence had saved my life, his head having screened me from the splinters from the grenade. But what grenade? A German one? Or was it rather the premature explosion of one of ours, one more on top of so many others?

I had the sensation that I had gone deaf. I could still hear our 155s firing, but the heavy triple detonation of a moment ago had suddenly become quite weak: one would have thought it was three sharp taps of a hammer on a sheet of metal. This comparative deafness unnerved me. But at the same time the voice of cowardice whispered, 'Perhaps it will get me sent back . . .' On this point, however, I was deceived, for the specialist I was sent to see a few days later, though he found that the ear-drum had been perforated, assured me that it would heal up of its own accord . . .

The following day seemed almost quiet, despite the artillery pounding which we had now grown accustomed to. True, nearly all the enemy shells fell too far behind us. On the other hand, our 75s fired sometimes too short. One of them wounded five or six of our men from the 125th in the arm or neck. They came to have their wounds dressed by the medical orderly without a moan, and I inwardly admired their passive submission to their fate. I personally would not have accepted this 'accident' with such resignation. This episode revived in me the infantryman's old resentment against guns and gunners.

XV

'WE GO BACK TONIGHT'

NIGHT fell. I no longer reckoned the number of days we had spent in the front line, nor our chances of being relieved. Suddenly we saw the ration party returning with their hands empty and bringing the great news, 'We go back to-night'. We who had come through leapt for joy. We were going to get out.

But then the Captain came and told me to explain to the men that we could not leave our dead in the trench and that we had to place them all together in the bare makings of a trench behind us, since we could not bury them. The thought of this task put me out of temper, but, however, I realized the need for it. How could we leave our successors with a trench full of corpses? And then, we owed this small honour to our unfortunate comrades.

I had difficulty in persuading our men, who were all exhausted—the reinforcements had already departed—but I had sufficient influence over them to make them see reason. In the light of the stars and the glow of the time-shells which exploded over our heads, we went from corpse to corpse. With a heavy heart we recognized the face of each man, although they were already remote and decomposing. We slipped each body on to a piece of canvas, which served both as a winding-sheet and a bier. The stench of flesh that was beginning to putrefy assailed the nostrils of the bearers in waves, and sometimes they had to stop and take a breath of fresh air before going on. We finally came to the end of this ghastly task, and I had the bitter satisfaction of having done what needed to be done.

At about 2 o'clock in the morning the relief-draft arrived. It was a company from the 410th. I was waiting for it at Company Headquarters. I watched the men file past, bowed down under the crushing weight of their packs, exhausted, bemused, leaving behind them the foetid smell of sweat. The Lieutenant to whom I passed on my orders proved peevish. As I showed him the trench which came under the enfilading fire of the German machine-guns, and which it was impossible to man, he swore and said:

'But where am I going to put my men? There'll never be enough room for them. And your sector's in a fine state! No grenades, no wire . . .'

I felt a sudden wave of anger at such injustice. Had we suffered so much just for this idiot to come and pretend that we had not done our job? And then my anger gave way to bitterness and a sense of irony. Who would ever know what we had done? Perhaps these very men who had come to relieve us would begin to understand in ten days' time, if they were still alive.

And so we left, in haste, for the day was not far distant and one could feel the fresh breeze which precedes the dawn.

We marched at a fast pace, going down the slopes and up the ridges with the same fervour. All the weariness of the previous ten days seemed to have vanished. After a stiff climb I called a halt, but at the end of a couple of minutes I

101

regretted that we were thus increasing the length of time we still had to pass in the danger area. 'Shall we move on?' I asked, and the men all leapt to their feet, as if they had the same thoughts as I did. A little farther on a 105 skimmed over our heads and burst twenty yards in front of us, and so we hurried on faster. The bare plateaux began to be outlined against the pale sky. It was dawn.

It was daylight when we reached the fort of Froideterre. I halted my men in the rear of the concrete walls, where they should be protected from a long-range salvo from the 105s. Along the bottom of a gully some new troops were climbing up towards us, their greatcoats bright blue, their tanned leather straps still yellow, their mess-tins gleaming like silver. Suddenly there was a whine, a cloud of white smoke which hid the group from us, and an explosion which dinned on our ears. When the cloud had dissipated we saw two of these fine brand-new soldiers stretched on the ground, while the remainder had scattered in every direction like a covey of partridges surprised by a gun-shot. 'Two knocked out,' coldly remarked one of the men, and we set off again, unconcerned.

We moved down towards the Meuse, following a muddy track made by the artillery wagons and field-kitchens and which had become enlarged with new ruts as the vehicles had moved to the side to avoid the old pot-holes. On the way we noticed signs of destruction: a blue-grey ambulance-lorry leaning over on its side, its left wheel shattered by a shell; a dead artillery-horse which stank; farther on, two corpses which were also putrefying beside the road. At last we reached the road for Bras. The men turned round from time to time to cast a wary eye up at a German sausage-balloon, 'that bastard who's observing the road and might easily send us over a packet'.

Here was Belleville Fort, with a battery of 75s barking sharply and angrily. Here was the Montgrignon crossroads with the first gendarme. On our right the silver Meuse flowed quietly between the meadows. Beyond was Verdun, red and white in the morning sun, silent and apparently dead among the hills, where our 75s were firing away while German 150s thundered down. War was beautiful, as seen by the generals, the journalists, and the academicians such as Henry Bordeaux or Louis Madelin.

We crossed the Galavaude bridge once more, and I watched the remains of the company file past—some thirty men out of one hundred and thirty. Most of them were without pack or belt, some of them did not even have their rifles. They moved on in a furtive, disorderly manner, as if they had fled from the battle. Their eyes were still feverish and their faces were weathered, their growth of beard matted with dirt. These heroes scarcely gave the appearance of heroes.

After crossing the bridge we found our field-kitchen and hot coffee and boiling soup, which we drank in the shelter of the embankment along which the road ran through the meadows beside the river. Truchet, our chief medical officer, was there, though he hardly recognized me under my ten days' growth of beard.

We set off once more and did not halt again until we had reached the edge of Thierville wood. The sausage-balloon which we had seen earlier floated above us, and we could make out the observer, a little black puppet in the gondola slung under the balloon's enormous beige belly. Near by, a working party of territorials was digging a gutter. Their sergeant was reading a newspaper. I asked him what the news was and he replied scornfully, 'Oh, it's always the same old thing,' and handed me the sheet. I looked through the official communiqué, and then cried with pride, 'That's us, that's us!' The men gathered round and I read out aloud:

'8th June, 23.00 hrs . . . On the right bank, the enemy, after a violent bombardment, directed successive attacks on our positions to the west and east of Thiaumont Farm. All the attacks were driven back by our barrage and machine-gun fire. . . . 9th June, 15.00 hrs . . . On the right bank the Germans continued to make violent attacks along a front of over one mile to the east and west of Thiaumont Farm . . . All the assaults to the west failed and the enemy suffered heavy losses. . . .'

'They don't speak of our losses,' one man muttered, but he was the only one to grumble. As to the rest, their eyes sparkled with pride, and they kept on repeating, 'That means us!' Man gains self-respect from his worst ordeals.

We finally reached Baleycourt. I went off on my own to the first houses in the village in search of our baggage train. I came upon a group of officers of light cavalry from the divisional squadron, with fawn-coloured riding boots, light blue uniforms, white-braided kepis cocked over one ear, close-shaven, pink and healthy. They seemed to belong to the front page of *La Vie Parisienne* and be ready to flirt with amiable patriotic ladies, as in the sketches by Hérouard which decorated the headquarters in various sectors. On seeing me they stopped dead, as if I were a ghost. In fact, with my crumpled leggings, the skirts of my great-coat matted with dried mud, my field-glasses dangling on my chest, my ten days' growth of beard, my eyes still feverish under my helmet which had lost its crest, I must suddenly have presented to these men favoured by war a living picture of the battle itself. I saluted them coldly and asked if they knew where the regimental transport was to be found as I wanted to take 'what remains of my company' to it. An embarrassed Lieutenant asked, 'How many of you are there?' When I replied, 'Thirty', I could see the look of alarm in their eyes. I was annoyed with myself afterwards for having gained an effect so easily by exploiting the death of others. But how could one resist giving a lesson to these favourites of fate.

Near Moulin-Brûlé I heard an engine whistle on the little local line of Bar-le-Duc. I had regained the world of peace and of life, and had escaped from the pillory of suffering. I thought I was the same man that I had been before those ten days passed face to face with death. I was wrong. I had lost my youth.

XVI

THE SAME AGAIN

O<small>N</small> leaving Verdun behind us we never thought that we should return. We expected to be sent into a quiet sector.

We had good reason to believe so. The losses of the two regiments in the brigade had been so heavy that the command had decided to form a single regiment with three battalions out of the two regiments—the 293rd and 337th—with their two battalions each, and to abolish our 337th regiment. We therefore had to change the numbers on the collars of our greatcoats and tunics and agree to wear the number 293, which we did not like. The companies had to be reorganized and the officers and N.C.O.s redistributed among them, while the men themselves were re-equipped. This meant that the new regiment was totally lacking in cohesion, since the majority of officers and N.C.O.s alike did not know their men. We considered that this new unit made up of bits and pieces would need weeks of training and 'taking in hand' before it could again be put in the front line.

Whereupon we suddenly received orders from General Mangin himself to return to the citadel that very evening 'in order to fill a gap'. The news came as a shock to those of us who had survived the ten days of hell at Thiaumont. I did my best to reassure the men, but scarcely succeeded in raising their morale. We followed exactly the same route that we had taken at the end of May: it was our second ascent to Calvary.... Everyone thought, 'You may come back once, but not twice!'

At the citadel the Commanding Officer gathered together the officers of the battalion. It was Lieutenant-Colonel Manceron, who, as a former Major on the General Staff, had managed to obtain authorization for us to go along the Voie Sacrée at the end of May, so as to reach our billets. Physically, he was the typical military man: lean and spare, with a bony face, clipped moustache, straight nose, piercing eyes, and grey hair brushed straight back. By his uprightness and courage he had quickly won over the officers and men of the battalion which he had commanded at Thiaumont. Promotion had led to his present command of the newly formed regiment.

Leaning over the map of the sector which covered the table in his narrow casemate, he announced that the regiment had orders to re-capture the Thiaumont redoubt, which had been lost since our first stay at the beginning of June. Then he added in a rather hoarse, jerky voice, almost between his teeth:

'Gentlemen, the task is a difficult one, but the situation is no longer the same as it was a month ago. The Boches have withdrawn most of their artillery and moved it up to the British front. Consequently, we shall be able to make a surprise attack without a gun-shot. Moreover, your battalion will be held in reserve and you may not even be called on to take part.'

I watched his jaws contract and form two folds under his thin cheeks. He was visibly trying to inspire in us a confidence that he did not feel himself. What could he expect of our awkward patched-up regiment, of our men getting on in years, most of them survivors from the hell of Verdun, neither whose strength nor morale were up to this? He must have known that we were going to the slaughter. But how could he say no to Mangin? He was in even less of a position to say no since he had not got behind him the experience of a regimental officer who had been in a number of 'shows', but of a staff-officer who had only recently left his desk and had still to prove himself.

On leaving the casemate which served as the Colonel's office, I noticed a crowd standing outside the door of another casemate, that of the battalion's assistant medical officer. Some fifty men were waiting their turn to plead to be sent to the rear. One complained of a hernia, another of rheumatism, yet another of bad feet or an old wound in the side. Through the open door I dimly made out stout Bayet, the medical officer, with his cropped head, his large spectacles, his brow gleaming with perspiration, struggling in the midst of his would-be sick, who hung on to him like drowning men clinging to a life-buoy.

A little later I learnt that some of the officers had acted in the same way: Meulen, great big Meulen, Chevalier of the Legion of Honour, who at Belval, before Verdun, had risen up in anger at the defeatist attitude of the chief medical officer, had just got himself returned to base by the same medical officer for heart disease; Beaurieux, who had been put up for the Legion of Honour after having spent the ten days at Thiaumont at the bottom of the only dug-out in the whole sector, staying there for even the most, let us say, *down to earth* needs, Beaurieux had informed the Colonel that, physically, he could not go on and that he must be sent to the rear. The Colonel, who up till then had had complete confidence in him, knowing nothing of his conduct at Thiaumont, had merely said, 'You, too, Beaurieux!' and turned his back on him. In short, it was a stampede.

The stampede was contagious. That evening I found myself alone for a moment with Dr Bayet and for his benefit I played a little comedy of which I was afterwards not very proud.

'Well,' I said, 'so you've sent a lot of them back?'

'Oh, good Lord, no! Eight of them turned up. Who'd have thought that? If one listened to them all there'd be no one at the front.'

'What do you expect? The example's set at the top—Meulen, Beaurieux. After all, everyone's got something. I myself, if I wanted to, could get myself sent to the rear. Look, feel my heart . . .'

I unbuttoned my tunic.

What mad hope had I that Bayet would say:

'My, my, just a moment . . . Let me sound your chest properly . . . But you can't go out there in that condition! I'll have you sent back as an emergency case!'

As if, even supposing that I were really sick, Bayet would have been able to reach a decision so quickly! But he merely said in a bored voice:

'Yes, perhaps you have got a slight murmur over the heart.'

'Well, there you see!' I said to save face, but I implied, 'I myself, if I wanted to . . .'

I buttoned up my tunic, somewhat put out by the failure of this timid attempt. But this sign of weakness stopped me thereafter from judging and condemning others.

Night came, we left the citadel, and at first we followed the route we had taken at the end of May: Verdun, Rue Mazel, the Galavaude bridge —how many of us would come back across that bridge?—and the suburbs of Belleville. Everything promised a repetition of our ordeal of the previous month.

But instead of taking the Bras road we turned to the right, passed close by the ruined church of Belleville and climbed the steep hill on which Belleville Fort stood, along a path bordered by shell-holes. I reached the top out of breath, my heart thumping, and when we halted I lay full length on the ground as if I were dead. I was exhausted, morally even more than physically exhausted. I was expecting to pass out, perhaps I was even hoping to . . . And then we set off again and finally arrived at a rough dug-out covered with corrugated iron at the end of a narrow approach trench. I fell asleep.

The following morning I took a look around. We were on the side of a little valley which opened on to Froideterre—Cold Earth was an apt name for it—a long bare ridge which extended from Fleury-devant-Douaumont down to the Meuse. All around us, except to the south, the view ended in a line of barren ridges. At the head of the valley we could see a grey concrete block, rectangular in shape, with here and there a door. This was fort MF 2, half buried in the ground, which served both as a command post and dressing-station.

On the other side of the valley a battery of 75s fired its four guns at regular intervals and one could hear the passionate whine of the four shells as they went on their way. Thereupon a salvo of

German 150s fell right on top of the battery, or so it seemed, sending up fountains of brown earth. One would have expected the French battery to be wiped out, but less than a minute later it sent off another salvo. This was followed by the arrival of another four 150s—and so it went on. For a long time we watched this artillery duel and were filled with admiration for the pluck of these gunners whom the enemy's heavy guns failed to silence. This episode reconciled us somewhat to the artillery.

Above our positions and near the ridge a few communication trenches somehow or other gave shelter to the men of the other battalions, who were waiting for nightfall to take up their advance positions ready for the attack. Shells burst from time to time on the farther side with their usual whine. One of them must have fallen right on top of a trench. I saw a figure rise up, silhouetted against the sky, and run screaming towards MF 2. So the Germans had not withdrawn much from their lines. . . . At this point I saw Captain Estève approaching from the 23rd, another company which had taken cover near the gallant battery of 75s. His feet dragged as he walked and his large body was slightly bent over his long legs. I admired his coolness. The remarks he made and the fact that he had been an N.C.O. in Africa earned him the reputation of being unconventional in matters of love—a charge, moreover, that he never defended himself against. Though he was thus condemned in the opinion of others for his predilections, when it came to the test this man displayed a calmness and courage which were strangely lacking in his more conventional brother officers. I expressed my admiration. He smiled, disclosing his beautiful white teeth under his brown moustache and screwed up his eyes like almonds between the long side-whiskers which ran down in front of his ears. With his usual African fatalism he remarked:

'Young 'un, what is written is written. Which reminds me, do you know that that old fool Major T..., who is due to attack tomorrow, has asked that a Lieutenant from our battalion should be attached to him for the assualt? It seems that the Colonel hesitated for a long time between you and my old friend Plantiveau. Finally Plantiveau was nominated for the job. The poor bugger has entrusted his walking-stick to his friend Robin, and when he left me he said good-bye in a mood of utter dejection. He had death in his eyes. You can see that he's telling himself that he won't return.'

I shudder in retrospect to think that the Colonel's choice could have fallen on me. Nonsense, as Estève used to say, what is written . . .

On the next day we were alerted at dawn. A runner out of breath brought us the yellow envelope which always used to make me tremble, for it contain our fate. We were to move forward immediately through the Quarries in order to reinforce the front line at Fort X. We knew neither the Quarries nor Fort X, but the runner was to be our guide. There was the usual commotion in preparing for battle. While some men hurriedly snatched a bite, others took great care to empty their bladder, for they had been told that a bullet in the belly was fatal if the bladder was full. We set out. On the way, men here and there told us the attack had failed. One could have expected as much.

We reached the Quarries and halted before a dug-out in which the Brigade General Staff was entrenched. On top of the gully up which we were climbing, 150s fell regularly and the wounded returning from the front line seemed to be playing hide-and-seek with the shells. A thoroughly scared Lieutenant came out of the dug-out and delivered a patriotic little speech:

'The attack has failed . . . Our losses are heavy . . . There is almost no one left up there . . . We must reform the line . . .'

He stopped a moment. He was clearly searching for the concluding phrase. Then he said:

'And now, keep up your courage!'

Thereupon he turned on his heel and returned to his dug-out, while we set off for the ridge, continually pounded by the 150s.

Those words 'Keep up your courage' in fact *discouraged* us, particularly when we learnt through the grape-vine which kept the men posted on everything that happened, that on seeing the 150s our Battalion Commander had suddenly discovered that he had pneumonia and he too had got himself sent to the rear.

Just before we reached the danger spot we again halted. At that moment some men were hit by shell-bursts. I admired the way in which in a flash they had got rid of their packs, equipment and rifles, keeping only their haversacks and gas-masks, and hurriedly decamped with their 'war wounds' to the rear and the prospect of living. One might have thought that they had learnt to become 'walking wounded' from their army manuals. Finally, we ran across between salvoes, half a section at a time, without incident.

In the shell-holes half filled with water on the ridge were the bodies of Frenchmen and Germans alike. In fact the Germans had advanced this far on 23rd June, and had been able to see the towers of Verdun Cathedral. One of them was so black that at first I wondered whether the Germans were recruiting African troops as we had done, but the familiar stench revealed that it was a white man undergoing putrefaction, and this reminded me of what I myself was likely to become in a few days' time.

At that moment a runner, out of breath, came and told us:

'Stay where you are! There are already too many men at Fort X, and nobody knows where to put them!'

We were in fact by Fort Y, a little steel wall covered with earth on the north side, an infantry redoubt dating from before the war. The entire company took cover behind it to escape the shells which were coming from the north—88s, 105s and 150s fell everywhere around us, but none on the fort itself. I opened a tin of beef and ate the excessively red meat and drank the purple commissariat wine. While eating this meal I calmly watched the worms which were wriggling around us and which came from a near-by corpse.

From time to time casualties passed along the path beside which we were crouched. A party of stretcher-bearers arrived from the rear. One of them was from the same village as one of my men. Having clapped each other on the shoulder and effusively expressed their pleasure at meeting with an exchange of 'You old bastard', 'You son of a bitch', one of them said:

'Well, there's been a real showdown up there.

Three colonels have copped a packet already this morning!'

'Don't let that worry you,' said the other, 'there's no shortage of colonels.'

We soon saw the three colonels, killed or wounded, brought back on stretchers. The third was Manceron. The four stretcher-bearers halted when they reached us. I was deeply affected when I recognized his ashen face. His head straight, his eyes closed, his arms lying alongside his body, he lay in his colourless greatcoat like a hero on his tomb. He died next day at the field-hospital.

I now heard details of this senseless morning attack. The assault troops had gone in in hopeless disorder, all the companies mixed up, and without a gun being fired in support. The German machine-guns had halted the brunt of the first wave in their tracks and killed or wounded the officers, who had been the first to leap out of the shell-holes in order to set an example. Thereupon the Germans had attempted to counter-attack. It was at this point that Manceron had rallied everyone around him—liaison N.C.O.s, telephone orderlies, signallers, sappers, all those in the headquarters wing whom we had treated as 'skrimshankers'—and he had gone out first in his calm, grave way. He had not advanced two paces before he received a bullet in the stomach and fell. Lieutenant Plantiveau had fallen beside him, mortally wounded. Thereafter no one had stirred, not a single rifle-shot was heard, and the stretcher-bearers had been able to pick up the Colonel's body undisturbed.

This sacrifice of a commanding officer whom we admired and whom we were beginning to love, grieved me deeply, but at the same time his example gave me some moral comfort after all the timidity and cowardice we had seen around us. And when the four stretcher-bearers, after spitting in the palms of their hands, lifted the stretcher up again and set off once more with their heavy measured pace, I noticed in the faces of my men a solemn look which bore witness to the force of this example.

A little later I saw Captain Keller go by. His company had been held in reserve but now, accompanied by a few men, he was moving up to the front line. When he had learnt of Plantiveau's death he had decided to go and find his body, not hesitating to desert his post in order to pay his last respects to our friend. As always he had on his plain light blue kepi, with no insignia, as stiff as a shako, and he wore an old tunic and a vast pair of dungaree trousers which flopped over his puttees. Between his lips hung his everlasting cigarette. He remained faithful to the eccentric character that he had created for himself. His little group returned shortly bearing the body rolled up in a piece of canvas from which a pair of feet in muddy gaiters stuck out. I can still see Plantiveau, with his broad forehead, his sad eyes and his iron-grey beard. This unassuming country solicitor who, it was said, had never smiled since his wife's death, used to devour the newspapers at the rest camp, jumping up and down when he came across articles full of patriotic hot air. He was a Protestant, and one day in the mess he had reacted violently when one of us had accused Protestantism of being cold and dismal and opposed to art, nature and living. I can still hear his voice trembling with anger as he shouted:

'I won't have anyone speaking like that!'

Thereafter we refrained from discussing religion in front of him. And now he had been killed, senselessly, uselessly, knowing that he was going to meet his death and giving, he too, an example of tacit obedience to the call of sacrifice.

As night was falling I saw Gaillard approaching, a former sergeant in the Paris fire-brigade and now a lieutenant in the 4th battalion, who had been reported killed during the attack that morning. I gave a sudden start when I saw this ghost. This great big fellow was walking about with his head bare except for a large white bandage which covered his right eye. He stumbled along, supported by an old stretcher-bearer. I went up to him and spoke my name. He turned his head back so as to be able to see me out of his left eye and said, his lips gummy with saliva:

'They got me, the bastards! But what I don't understand is that mine was supposed to be the left assault company of the left battalion and we turned out to be the right company of the right battalion. . . .'

He was obsessed by this and he repeated the remark two or three times—a remark that said much for the disorder in which this appalling attack had been launched.

'But why do you make him walk?' I asked the stretcher-bearer in an undertone. 'Aren't there any more stretchers?'

'He doesn't want to lie down. What can I do about it?' Then, turning to Gaillard, he said, 'Come on, sir. Let's keep going.'

The wounded man set off again, a tragic figure in the dark night.

Later we received orders to move over to our

right to relieve a company in the front line, which an orderly came to guide us to. We went back along the path which had led us up to Fort Y. We reached the danger spot which we had run across between salvoes of 105s. No shells were falling for the moment, but in my mind's eye I saw the barrels of the German guns standing out against the night sky, ready to open fire again along the same co-ordinates. 'Hurry up, hurry up!' I said to my men, 'this is a bad patch.' At that precise moment a column arrived which was about to cross our path.

'Halt, there!' I shouted. 'Let us pass!'

'What? It's for us to pass!' replied an arrogant voice.

'No, but you can't. We're going up to the front.'

'What the hell's that got to do with it? We're going up too. I'll bar your way if I have to.'

'Do you know who you're speaking to?'

'No. Do you? I'm Major Berteaux of the 130th, and I'll ask you to bloody well get out of my way!'

I shut up, completely paralysed. What could a lieutenant do against a major? The column filed past in front of us while I fretted. After that we hurried on, for daylight was not far off.

I met the Captain I was to relieve at the bottom of a shell-hole. He was bearded and cheerful, and he gave me a hearty welcome:

'Ah, you've come to replace us? Well, it's not a bad stretch here. The Boches shell us like mad, but everything falls behind us in the Ravine des Vignes. During the day you can't stick your nose above ground. There are machine-guns at Command Post 119 which will settle your hash in a jiffy. No trench, just shell-holes where the men crouch down in threes or sixes. Actually, you'll find it's not too bad. The worst part's getting here. You're forced to follow that God-awful narrow-gauge railway in the gully so as not to get lost. The whole way along it's bordered with shell-holes made by 210s. And not a bit of shelter except for a few gunners' dug-outs. If you're caught by a barrage the only thing to do is to fling yourself into a shell-hole and hope that the gun that made it has altered its aim a bit since the last shot. . . . Well, that's war. There's no point in worrying about it. If you're killed, the war's over for you. If you're wounded? You've got Biarritz and the dear young things from the Red Cross. The biggest bore, after all, is to come through. Then you've every chance of going on doing this God-awful job. Well, good-bye and good luck! I'm off, for it's beginning to get bloody light.'

So this man who was so devil-may-care, or at least pretended to be in order to overcome his fears, ambled off towards the Ravine des Vignes.

I spent two days at the bottom of this shell-hole made by a 210, which was at least habitable. The bottom had been flattened out and the circumference had been provided with little traverses made of clods of earth—there being no sand-bags available. On our right rose Souville Fort. My 1/80,000 map (we had nothing on a smaller scale) said that I ought to be able to see the village of Fleury-devant-Douamont. I searched for it, but in vain. At last I noticed a few whitish specks against the background of brown clay. These were the few bits of rubble which were all that remained of the village, which was occupied by the Germans.

We lived peacefully in these shell-holes, beneath the whine of the shells that fell behind us. There was little to relieve the boredom. We watched our Nieuports turning in the blue sky—proof that the mastery of the air had at last changed sides. We defended ourselves against the swarms of green flies which were attracted by the left-overs in our mess-tins and by the near-by corpses. At night I would creep from shell-hole to shell-hole in order to visit my men. 'So all the officers are buggering off, are they?' one of them flung at me, for they were all aware that Meulen, Beaurieux and the Major had been evacuated. 'Not all, since I'm here,' was the only answer I could give. Whereupon the man replied: 'I wanted to be sent back too, and you know what the Major said to me? "You bloody malingerer, bugger off and get back to your company. There's nothing the matter with you. You'll go up the line like the rest."'

It was among these shell-holes that one of my men told me one of the best war stories that I know. The scene is a quiet sector where there has been a great deal of rain. The boyaux are full of mud and as night is falling the ration parties, despite orders to the contrary, walk along the path that runs along the top of the trenches. One of these parties goes by, swinging the dixies and mess-tins. From the bottom of the trench, along which some soldiers are laboriously making their way, sinking into the mud up to their ankles at every step, an authoritative voice calls out:

'What are you doing up there?'

'What do you mean? Can't you see we're the ration party?'

'Why don't you go along the trench?'

'Ha! That's a good one! Do you think we're such bloody fools as to march through the mud like you?'

'This is the General speaking . . .'

'The General? He's not such a c... as to come out here at this time of night!'

The General decided it was better not to labour the point.

It was a strange thing, but normally the great pyramid of military authority weighed heavily on me and I grew impatient with all the blind obedience. But in this advanced post, two or three hundred yards from the Germans, cut off from the rear by the almost continuous enemy bombardment, I felt myself more independent of my commanding officers than ever before. Here in the front line I was the master next to God, like the captain of the ship in the heart of the storm. While in my shell-hole, I received an order, tied to a bundle of cartridges, to make a surprise attack on Command Post 119, taking advantage of an assault on Fleury which a neighbouring regiment was to attempt the next day. I contented myself with a burst of derisive laughter. I was the sole judge of the possibilities and the chances of success, and it was I who would finally decide. . . . Moreover, the attack on Fleury must have been postponed. In any case, it did not take place while we were in the sector.

The return to the rear was without incident. We hurried along the narrow-gauge railway in constant fear of a burst of 105s or a salvo of 210s. In the gully where Fort MF 2 stood, fires glowed on both slopes, as if the place were lit up for the occasion. At first a mad idea entered my head—were they celebrating the 14th of July? But on thinking about it I realized it was only the 11th. When we had advanced a bit farther I learnt that a German shell had blown up an ammunition dump containing cartridges, grenades and flares. Everything had burnt, exploded and gone up in the air and the burning flares had fallen all over the gully, setting the straw roofs of some temporary stables on fire. We naturally made jokes about this fire display, as if it had been arranged in our honour.

I remained unmoved by the various halting-places which had now become familiar to me—Montgrignon, the Galavaude bridge, Souville Wood. I was still in that pleasant state of indifference in which one knows neither hope nor fear, and which, as I have already said, is probably the ideal condition for the soldier.

XVII

THE OFFENSIVE OF 16th APRIL 1917 AND ITS CONSEQUENCES

W^E spent the winter of 1916–17 in and around Rheims. The various sub-sectors were Le Linguet, Laon railway line and Bétheny.

I remember little of my stay at Le Linquet, where the Company Headquarters were located in the ruins of a chemical factory surrounded by muck-carts from Rheims itself—fortunately odourless after two years during which time they had not been used. I can clearly recall of the Laon railway line. The track ran across the plain on an embankment, and my dug-out (in the second line of defence) had been excavated in the embankment itself and was right underneath the rails. The morning after my arrival a spick and span staff-officer approached me and introduced himself in a rather strange manner:

'I'm Major X, on General Pétain's staff.'

I was a little surprised at this personal publicity, but I did not show it.

Thereupon the Major began to give me a thorough dressing down for the gaps in my barbed wire defences, without once letting me open my mouth. I had to wait till he had finished his indictment of me before I was able to point out to him that I had arrived the evening before and that it would have been difficult for me to complete the network in one night. Furthermore, barbed wire was being sent up from the rear only in driblets.

The Major was not to be put off by this and carried on with his tale about the need for additional defence. I looked with hatred on this armchair planner, who was clearly unaware of the practical difficulties in the face of which we regimental officers had to carry on.

At the time I very much regretted that I had not put into force in my sector a procedure which a friend of mine had applied with regard to staff-officers. He had given his men strict orders that any officer arriving in the lines who did not belong to the sector, should be brought to him between an escort of two men with fixed bayonets. As was to be expected, the officer with his blue, red or tricolour armband was usually fuming with rage. My friend then spoke to him coldly but courteously:

'I regret to have to force these formalities on you, sir, but not having been forewarned of your visit I must request you to show me your papers. As I am sure you know, spies have been reported in this sector, some of them, as it so happens, disguised as staff-officers, and I have not the honour of knowing who you are.'

The staff-officer would look daggers, but he had to show his papers, and the regimental officers were avenged. It is scarcely necessary to add that after two or three incidents of this nature, these gentlemen from the General Staff did not fail to announce their visits to my friend in advance—or simply preferred to avoid him.

I passed many a long week at Bétheny, a small village which then enjoyed a certain celebrity, since a great military review had been held there for the Tsar Nicholas II during his French visit before the war. We kept ourselves warm by sawing up and burning the old beams from the houses demolished by the bombardments. One of the positions intended to hold the Germans should they attack was in the cemetery, in a corner of which a concrete look-out post had been built, which, for all I know, still stands there. A brother officer said to me one day: 'Who knows? Perhaps Bétheny cemetery will one day become as famous in military history as that at Eylau or Saint-Privat!' I replied that, as long as I was there, I would much prefer this humble cemetery to remain inglorious, for my thirst for adventure had left me. I had had my fill at Verdun.

The Rheims sector was indeed a strange one. The general air of calm reigning over the region was occasionally broken by a few shells or a surprise attack launched for the purpose of taking prisoners. Each time the assault was prepared in advance by a heavy bombardment, a proper downpour of shells. As we had been officially informed of the cost of firing a 75-mm. gun and a 155-mm., we calculated that to capture one prisoner it was necessary to spend 300,000 francs. (These were gold francs, for we had not yet learnt to differentiate between gold and paper francs. and in answer to the appeals from above I had just turned in to the paymaster the five or six golden louis which my people had given me for the journey when I left them in 1914, and I had been given notes in exchange.) As Lieutenant Georges Robin remarked, at 300,000 francs per prisoner the Boche was costing a lot per ounce, and we asked ourselves who was going to pay for it all?

The city of Rheims, which lay within the second line of defence, that is to say, well within the fighting area, had not, however, been completely evacuated by the civilian population. Whether resting or held in reserve we went into billets. In one of these, an abandoned house in Rue Wehrlé, I had discovered a gramophone and a few records, and I listened with delight to the famous arias from the *Cavalleria Rusticana*, in the absence of Beethoven or Wagner. We courted the shop assistants of a department store, *La Poire d'Or*, in the centre of the town. Once assured of a good supper and a good night's lodging, we could go and look for the rest in a house of ill repute by the name of Triquenot. Since the trains, however, did not run as far as Rheims itself, when we went on leave we turned up at the Place Royale in our best uniforms and red kepis and took one of the fiacres which stood peacefully at the rank, as far as Bezannes, the rail-head for the Paris train —and all this only a couple of miles from the Germans.

When spring came, things deteriorated. At the end of 1916 Joffre had been discreetly removed and his place had been taken by General Nivelle. The success that Nivelle had achieved in re-taking certain key-positions among the Verdun advance posts had led to the belief that he was the man for the break-through, for the great liberation offensive. At the beginning of April we knew that the attack would not be long delayed. The increased activity of the artillery and the air corps must have already forewarned the enemy. At Bétheny I was relieved by a regiment from another division, and the Lieutenant who took over from me showed me the orders that he had already received for the offensive. He said with a note of irony in his voice: 'On the evening of D-day we are to be at Rethel, the following evening at Novion-Porcien, and the day after that at Mézières—as if there weren't any Germans on the other side!' From that moment I was able to gauge the difference between this offensive and that in Champagne on 25th September 1915. Now, the men were no longer in the mood. Furthermore, as the days went by our artillery pounding seemed to slacken, as if we were running short of ammunition, whereas the German artillery increased its counter-bombardment. To crown it all, we learnt that a company sergeant-major or a warrant-officer ordered to carry out a surprise attack in the Sapigneul region had failed to take the precaution of leaving his papers behind him. He had been taken prisoner and the Germans had thus had G.H.Q.'s detailed orders for D-day delivered right into their hands. In short, everything promised a fiasco.

We were held in reserve, in Rheims itself. As the town was being shelled more heavily we were no longer billeted in the houses, but in the cellars of the champagne establishments. Of course, these cellars were empty and the stocks of precious bottles were carefully stowed away in other cellars and kept under lock and key. Those civilians who had not wished to be evacuated were cooped up in the cellars next to ours; so that while the German 150s and 210s were bursting over our heads we were able to flirt with their daughters. We sang the song of the day, which I accompanied by scraping away on a wretched violin:

Spring is in the air,
You can see them by the Thames,
Walking pair by pair,
The lads with their lady friends.

We had discovered a magnificent source for supplying the officers' mess with wine—the private cellar of the owner of the champagne establishment where we were quartered. This cellar was locked up, but to its great misfortune it received the light of day through a small circular window. Before each meal a detachment of two or three officers passed down the corridor leading to this cellar and thrust a tiny little Captain, a Chevalier of the Legion of Honour (at this period the Legion of Honour was rare and had not yet been devalued) head first through the circular window. He was held securely by the legs until he had found a firm position with his hands. Then he took his electric torch out of his pocket and asked: 'What would you like today? A 1908 Pommard? A 1911 Château-Margaux? A 1913 Corton?' For there was every kind of wine there, except champagne. We would choose two or three bottles which the Captain would then pass to us through the window, and then we extracted him from the cellar by the same route. If the cellar did not cave in under the gun-fire, the poor owner must have received a very distressing surprise on his return. Although we had not actually broken in, this case of looting would certainly have appeared reprehensible in the eyes of a strictly moral person. But under the hail of German 150s and 210s then breaking over the town and threatening to flatten everything, even the cellars, our ideas of right and wrong were no

128

longer very clear. And everybody knows that the French soldier thinks that he has a right to every bottle of wine within his reach. In his own mind he thinks: 'How can society refuse me these small favours when it demands that I should be ready to give up my life for it?'

What did annoy me was that one fine evening this same Captain who performed these 'samplings', stood at the entrance to the cellar where our men were quartered and confiscated the bottles that some of them had 'found' in the cellars in the neighbourhood. I naïvely considered that the law should be the same for all, and that it was difficult for us to forbid our men from doing what we practised ourselves. The Captain was clearly not of this opinion. If anyone had criticized him he would doubtless have retorted by reminding us of the need for discipline and the danger of drunkenness. But I knew him well enough to realize that he considered the common law was not made for him. In a rather over-simple way, I classified him as right-wing while I considered myself left-wing.

D-day finally arrived. It was 16th April 1917. As on 25th September 1915, the attempt at a break-through failed, with heavy losses, and we had to carry on with our life in the trenches, sentry-duty and nightly rounds, bombardments and surprise attacks, regularly interspersed with rest periods in Rheims. But this new set-back had consequences which had not been foreseen. One evening as we were waiting in the front line for the officers of the battalion which was due to relieve us, we received a telephone call to say that the relief had been postponed for twenty-four hours. This was fairly unpleasant news for men who had just completed ten days in the front line. The officers of the relief-draft eventually arrived the following evening, and what they had to say dumbfounded us. They had only just managed to come at all, for their men had presented them with a list of demands, like so many workmen addressing their employer, and agreed to go up the line only if these were acceded to. They demanded the resumption of furlough, improvement in the standard of food, immediate surrender of their gratuity books by means of which they were forced to save, etc. We could not believe our ears. They added that at Rheims they had seen soldiers loitering about who had come from God knows where and who had confabulated with our men from the Vendée and worked on their feelings.

This was the manner in which we learnt of the critical state of morale in the French army at that time. In our regiment matters went no further. By temperament and tradition the people of the Vendée are amenable and respect their leaders. But we knew that certain regiments had mutinied, that it had been found necessary to make examples and shoot the ringleaders. We also knew that the officers had often had to bear a large share of the responsibility. In these regiments, at rest camps or held in reserve near Paris, the officers went off every evening without special permission to join their wives or mistresses in Paris, while they threatened any ordinary soldier who tried to do likewise, with the ordeal of a court-martial. Now, the French have a passion for equality beyond all measure, and the men refused to accept that they should be denied the freedom that their officers enjoyed.

Before 1940, it was customary to credit General Pétain with having succeeded in allaying this crisis in the army's morale in 1917 in the most human way possible. Since 1944, political passions have induced some people to contest the part played by Pétain in this affair. I am able to offer only the modest evidence of a junior regimental officer. On every grand occasion, such as New Year's Day, 14th July, the anniversary of our entry into the war, etc., we received from General Headquarters an official message from the Supreme Commander, which we were supposed to read out to our men. This literary bombast nearly always seemed to me more dangerous than useful. I knew my men, I knew what had to be said to them, and I also knew what must not be said to them. So I took the liberty of censoring the text from G.H.Q., of cutting out this or that paragraph and of reading to the assembled company only what in my opinion would get across to them and would not serve to lower their morale. But the only general whose messages I was always able to read out in their entirety, and consequently the only one who in my eyes knew exactly how to speak to the French soldier, because he was the only one who knew him well, was Pétain.

We came across the final repercussions of this crisis a few months later when we were in reserve in the region of Noyon. A theatrical company touring the troops was to give a performance on an improvised stage in the open air on 19th July. The star of the cast was Marie Delna, an actress who had once been a great success, who had retained her beautiful voice, but who, alas, had grown appallingly fat as she became older and was indeed positively enormous. General Des Vallières, who commanded our division, welcomed the business manager, glanced at the programme and expressed his surprise that it did not end with the *Marseillaise*. The manager replied that they had learnt from bitter experience that in the present state of low morale it was better to avoid singing the French National Anthem in front of the troops. The General, who was a gallant man—he was killed by a German sniper while stepping out of his headquarters on 27th May 1918, during the enemy's break-through at Chemin-des-Dames—replied haughtily that such precautions were perhaps justified in the case of some troops but certainly not of his division. He could vouch for it. He quoted the example of another performance which had been given at the Rheims theatre a few weeks earlier, in which Madeleine Roch, the great tragic actress of the Comédie-Française, had declaimed the *Marseillaise* without the slightest disturbance and had been wildly applauded. The manager therefore reluctantly gave way.

So at the end of the performance Marie Delna came on to the stage in a white dress with the Tricolour in her hand and sang the *Marseillaise*. When she had finished, the applause she received was mixed with an outburst of hissing from the mass of soldiers. The General was livid and ordered the booers to be traced—an impossible task, of course. He had clearly been wrong in not relying on the manager's experience. The latter could sense the audience's feelings and knew that the *Marseillaise* ran the risk of being guyed, especially when sung by an actress as round as a barrel, and in the open air. The example of the

Rheims Theatre did not hold. The acting profession are well aware of the difference between an indoor and an open-air theatre and how difficult it is to catch and hold an audience out of doors. In any case the incident proved that the evil virus which had appeared in the army after the set-back of 16th April had not completely vanished and that it was still necessary to handle the men with care.

XVIII

A CHANGE OF REGIMENT AND
THE RESULTING DIFFICULTIES

AT the beginning of December 1917, we learnt that, as a result of the great decline in its fighting strength, our regiment was to be disbanded. The two regiments making up our brigade had already been amalgamated after Verdun. Once more we were going to have to change the number on our lapels. But the General Staff did not wish to lose entirely the sense of cohesion which had grown up between us and break up into a thousand bits and pieces what had become a staunch unit. Though the regiment was disbanded, each company with its arms and baggage was transferred to another regiment where it replaced one of the latter's companies. This company in turn was split up among the other companies in the regiment.

So it came about that I was sent with my men to join the nth reserve regiment in the north. This regiment bore the red and green colours of the Croix de Guerre, which meant that the regiment itself had twice been mentioned in dispatches. To us who knew about these things, this meant that on at least two occasions it had come through very severe fighting with honour and heavy losses. Those of us who fought in the 1914–18 War and are still alive today are somewhat irritated when on grand occasions we see the Paris police bearing the red colours which were awarded them at the time of the Liberation. These red colours used to be restricted to crack regiments which had been six times mentioned in dispatches. (Between the colours of the Croix de Guerre and those of the Legion of Honour came the yellow colours of the Military Medal, presented in the case of four mentions.) This signal honour was perhaps awarded somewhat precipitately to the police for its two hundred men killed in August 1944, who redeemed some of the pusillanimity of the period of occupation. Inflation devalues everything, decorations as much as money.

Though this retention of the original companies of the disbanded regiment had its advantages, it also had its drawbacks. We were not made very welcome in the battalion, one of whose companies we had replaced. A regiment disbanded was a regiment under suspicion: if we had been dispersed, it was doubtless because we were of little worth, perhaps we had even mutinied. When we arrived to join our new regiment behind Poperinghe in Belgium, we met an ox of a man from the 8th, somewhat the worse for drink, who on seeing our regimental number said, 'So you're the defectors'. We were intruders in this division, in which all the regiments had been presented with colours for gallantry. And our men from the Vendée were very different from the northerners of the other companies.

The officers of my new battalion themselves for the most part treated me with a certain lack of cordiality. I had been promoted captain in August, at the age of twenty-four, which was then fairly common in the infantry where an officer's fate could only be promotion or death, but this is no longer surprising today when we have seen generals under the age of thirty and the distribution of gold braid has become wanton. But my arrival with three gold bands on my arm in a battalion where I was to replace a lieutenant, seriously affected the ambitions of other lieutenants who were Company Commanders and had dreams of becoming captains. For although we were reservists, the war had been going on for so long that we now had the mentality of regular officers and, had there been an Army List, we would have savagely crossed off the names of the dead who brought us nearer the next rank up. Now, if a battalion had one captain commanding one of its four companies, the General Staff judged this sufficient and did not trouble to promote any others. So my arrival blocked the promotion of my brother officers, and at the battalion mess they gave me a pretty poor welcome.

Moreover, I landed up with a regiment in which the atmosphere was rather unpleasant. I had left behind a Battalion Commander whom I liked—Major Kreyser, who met a heroic death at Noyon six months later—and for whom I would have laid down my life. He was a regular officer who wished to persuade me to join the regular army. 'A captain at twenty-four, you have a brilliant military career before you. You'll go straight to Staff College. Because don't you have any illusions—however this all ends up, there'll always be Germans, and we'll always need an army.' His influence over me was so great that I almost put in a request for a permanent commission. But then, I thought, I was only an acting captain and at the end of the war I might be demoted. At the last moment I decided not to renounce the university career that had been promised me.

It was a good thing I did. My new regiment consisted of a bunch of rotters. Everyone ran down his brother officer, and the adjutant, who in civilian life owned a Paris bar, thought he could establish his influence over the Colonel by running down everyone else. The only person I could trust, Lacoste, a former student from the college I had been on the point of going to in 1914, put me on my guard against the pitfalls which I was about to come across. On his advice I bought a duplicate notebook in which I kept copies of all my reports and accounts so as to be able to cover myself in the case of any false accusations. The army life I had known with Major Kreyser had seemed as friendly and enjoyable as this now appeared hostile and detestable. I had the impression that I was living in one of those Italian states of the fifteenth century, in which one was forever expecting to be stabbed by a bully.

I also had to face other difficulties. The disbanding of the regiment had suddenly winkled from out of their holes a fair number of 'skrimshankers' who had had soft jobs away from the heavy fighting—colonel's groom, general's batman, colonel's cook, quartermaster sergeant and so forth. It had been necessary to assign all these fellows to the various companies, and for my part I had inherited a good thirty of them. It is easy to imagine the standard of morale of men who, since the outbreak of war, had been privileged to avoid the front line and who had hardly ever had more than an occasional heavy shell on their tails to remind them that we were fighting.

Moreover, their military training was appallingly deficient. They just about knew how to fire a rifle, for they had learnt that during their military service, but they were completely ignorant of the advances that had been made in the art of killing one's fellow-creatures which had been made since the war began, notably the use of the hand grenade. Grenades scared them. They had so often heard of premature explosions and the terrible wounds received by grenade-throwers! I had to take their training in hand and, taking advantage of the long weeks we spent at rest camps or in reserve, make soldiers out of them once more.

The grenade-throwing exercises were an ordeal for the men and for me alike. I had to take charge myself, go into the throwing trench with the soldiers to be instructed, take up the grenade and pull out the pin in order to show them that there was plenty of time to hurl it over the parapet before it exploded. After that I would place a grenade in the trembling hand of one of them and watch him warily, always afraid that in his emotion he would drop the unpinned grenade in the bottom of the trench, which would have been a radical way of ending the war for both of us.

And then these rather ungainly men (most of them were over thirty) had to be trained in attack and assault. On this score I had to draw the attention of the Colonel—who was at the end of his tether—to the fact that the average age of my men was appreciably higher than that of the men in the other companies. In short, I had a lot to do to incorporate the newcomers into the remains of my old company. And in spite of all my efforts, my men contined to be out of favour.

This was all the more so as I could hardly be

said to get on well with my Battalion Commander. He was a gaunt man with a bony face
and high cheek-bones, who prided himself on
being very athletic. Before the war he had
attended a number of courses at the Ecole de
Joinville, and eventually became an instructor
there. He did not like me, probably because in
his eyes I was an 'intellectual', and I made him
feel it. Various incidents arose between us which
did nothing to bring us together.

In the spring of 1918 we moved to Picardy,
going on foot in the heavy, stormy heat. The day's
march never exceeded ten miles, but nevertheless
it was a laborious trek. When we reached our
halting-place we usually had to wait until the
advance party had finished getting our billets
ready, that is, assigning barns to the various
companies and the available rooms to the officers.
As the men were always extremely thirsty, as soon
as they had piled their rifles they flew off into the
village like a flight of sparrows in search of water
or, better still, wine. The Major quite rightly grew
annoyed with this lack of discipline, and as we set
out on one occasion he gave strict instructions
that the men should stand by their piled rifles in
case the billets were not ready on our arrival. All
went as usual, and as soon as they had piled their
rifles I found the men growing impatient, saying
that they were dying of thirst. I considered the
Major's orders were far too strict and inhuman,
and so I called the duty sergeant and told him to
take a party of two men from each section with
all the water-bottles in order to fetch water. 'And
if anyone asks you who gave you permission,' I
added, 'say that it was me.' Just as I came to the
end of the sentence I felt something breathing

down my neck—it was the Major's horse. The Major had in fact come up behind me without my noticing and had heard everything. 'Captain Arnaud,' he burst out in a rage, 'I command this battalion, not you!' and he went on in this way saying that he would report me to the Colonel. However, my men stared at him with their eyes full of hatred and must have been grumbling to themselves. I was playing a fine part as far as my men were concerned, and I could even have been suspected of acting the demagogue since I was taking their side against orders that were too severe. I remained at attention, silent and pale. The incident had no consequences, for, I learnt later, the Colonel had a very poor opinion of the Major.

Another incident, this one comical, brought about my ultimate discredit in the eyes of my immediate superior. We were at a rest camp in the region of Rethondes—which was yet to achieve notoriety as the place where the Armistice was signed—and a sports day had been arranged to amuse the troops. The star turn was to be the Major, who was to plunge into the Oise from the top of the Rethondes bridge, 'fully armed and equipped', said the programme, 'so as to demonstrate that the true soldier must know how to handle a situation under any circumstances'. When the great moment arrived we gathered round the bridge. The Divisional Commander himself had deigned to honour the occasion with his presence. The Major turned up wearing an old tunic and a wretched pair of trousers, with a carbine slung over his shoulders. The bluffer, who had promised to be 'fully armed and equipped', had selected the lightest weapon and clothes. He mounted the parapet above one of the piers of the bridge and began to take several slow, deep breaths: I can still see his cheeks swelling and contracting rhythmically. Suddenly, plop! a soldier who was standing a few yards away among a group of spectators threw himself into the river. After a moment's astonishment the Major followed suit, and cried across the water, 'Shall I come to your assistance?' 'No thanks, sir,' the other replied, 'I'm quite all right,' and he swam back to the bank with a perfect overarm stroke. He had thus stolen the Major's thunder. The latter came out of the water in his turn, absolutely furious as one can well imagine. He asked whose company this practical joker belonged to and was told the 21st. That was mine.

The Major must have imagined, I am quite convinced of it, that I had promised a small reward to one of the men who was a good swimmer, if he would throw himself in the water first and ruin the effect of the demonstration. In actual fact, I learnt what had really happened from one of my sergeants—those invaluable intermediaries between officers and their men, as indispensable as the foremen in a factory who serve as a link between the management and the workmen. As the men were discussing the afternoon's programme that morning while waiting for lunch by the field-kitchen, one of them had bet a bottle of wine that he would dare to leap into the water before the Major, and he had won his wager.

I did not bother to repeat the story to my superior officer, who must have gone on crediting me with all sorts of dark designs. And my company remained in disgrace. But I was soon to have my revenge.

141

XIX

HALTING THE GERMAN
OFFENSIVE OF 27th MAY 1918

I^T is well known that on 27th May 1918 the German army delivered us a staggering blow: in a few hours it had broken through our lines at the Chemin-des-Dames and had quickly advanced from the Aisne to the Marne. The surprise was total. I have already mentioned that our former Divisional Commander, General Des Vallières, was killed that day by a German sniper while he was coming out of his headquarters far behind the front line. It was also said that a colonel in the Medical Corps had been taken prisoner at Fismes, and this misadventure to a high-ranking medical officer in the rear came to have a symbolic significance.

On 27th May itself I was returning from leave and I had trouble in rejoining my regiment, which I had left in Picardy. Each morning I would set out from Paris for one of the regulating stations where I learnt that my regiment had moved towards the east. I would return to Paris in the afternoon and set off again for another station next day. It was clear that the General Staff was 'castling' so as to place our reserves on the right flank of the German attack. It was only after three or four days, and with the aid of a meat-van—also of symbolic significance—that I succeeded in regaining my men near Villers-Cotterets. As I had arrived wearing my best uniform—the wagon with my uniform-case was God knows where—and there was no question of my going into battle in a red kepi and white gloves like the officers from the Military College in August 1914, I had to borrow a helmet from my sergeant-major, a quiet schoolmaster who was moving to the rear at the very moment when we were about to advance. And so I took up my command again.

For two or three days we marched and counter-marched through the district, without of course understanding what we were doing. We hung around the edge of the forest of Villers-Cotterets, near the farm of Vertefeuille, where we remained waiting a whole day. From time to time a heavy German shell landed on us, one of them seriously wounding my friend Lacaste, and I learnt how demoralizing it is to be bombarded under trees: the shells seemed to fall haphazardly without one's being able to locate the danger zone, and the vault of the trees reverberated with the thunderous sound of the explosion.

During these first days of June 1918, the army offered the spectacle of a remarkable mixture of control being lost and order being regained. At Vertefeuille, on the main road to Soissons, one saw unattached soldiers making for the south. They had 'lost their regiment', they said—and I remembered with bitter irony the fun we had had in the mess on discovering this phrase at the top of the list of common expressions in a little French–Italian dictionary. But at a crossroad a staff-officer stopped every man and told him in which direction he would find his unit.

From the edge of our forest we also saw a regiment make a counter-attack, moving towards a road planted with trees which were being swept by gun-fire: the men advanced in single column, in perfect order, as if on parade. Our airmen attacked the enemy aeroplanes incessantly. In short, one had the feeling that after the surprise of 27th May the army had made a rapid recovery. But it had been a near thing, and the proof of this was to be seen in the fact that it had been found necessary to use as infantry the cavalry that was still been held carefully in reserve 'for the break-through'.

We had in fact to relieve a troop of cavalry when we went up the line on the night of 2nd–3rd June. This was the strangest relief that I had ever taken part in. Around midnight our guides led me to three officers of dragoons who had gathered together at the foot of a tree in the midst of the battlefield, while my sections went off to replace their platoons. I had been told that we would be held in reserve. We introduced ourselves all round, and I secretly noted the contrast between the lengthy names of the noble families of the cavalry officers and my own humble surname, typical of an infantry officer. I asked them then what troops were in the line in front of us and who were holding our left and right flanks. They replied coldly that they had no idea. I had to send runners off immediately to my four section leaders to warn them that they might be in the front line and to keep their eyes skinned.

After that, these dragoons told me how their regiment had attacked during the day, on foot of course, and had been halted by the machine-guns. Their losses had been heavy.

'But they told us that our attack had been of great assistance to another operation farther north.'

As a soured and disillusioned infantryman, I admired the cool way in which these cavalry officers, after some four years of war, could retain the naïvety of August 1914. Admittedly, they had not been through the blood-baths of the grand offensives, since they had been kept back for the break-through.

They added that, in accordance with the orders received to maintain the cavalry spirit, they had charged with their lances at the ready.

I almost choked with anger. To think that in June 1918 one should send dragoons on foot, with their lances at the ready, against the German machine-guns would have been ludicrously funny if it had not also been tragic, for the following morning we were to see the numbers of dead bodies of unfortunate dragoons who had fallen on top of their lances.

Eventually the cavalry officers took their leave and wished me good luck. They went off taking with them the remains of their men to rejoin their horses, which were waiting for them in a valley slightly in the rear. But many a horse was without its rider.

I fell fast asleep on the bare earth. Early in the morning my Lieutenant, Georges Robin, woke me up with a start. 'They're bombarding us,' he said. 'Let's get moving.' Indeed, the 77s were falling all around us in the orchard where we found ourselves. Fortunately, a good number of these shells must have been badly made—*schlecht und billig*—for they did not explode. Nevertheless, we made our way towards the houses of the village of Mosloy, some sixty or seventy yards in our rear.

At the top of a flight of steps leading down to a cellar we saw a stout infantry company sergeant-major, a fine old man he seemed—he must have been forty at least—wearing the number 121 on his lapels, a regiment we had not heard of. He looked at me unsympathetically—old sergeant-majors scarcely approved of young captains—and told me that his Commanding Officer was down in the cellar. I went down and introduced myself, and told this Battalion Commander that my guides must have led me astray since I was lost in this sector of the wrong division, and added:

'My company is out there, on the outskirts of the village. I don't think there is anything better I can do than to place myself at your disposal.'

The Major thanked me. Suddenly the stout sergeant-major rushed down the steps with surprising agility and said:

'Sir, the Boches are attacking with tanks.'

'Good God!' exclaimed the Major. 'Let's get the hell out of here.'

And with one rapid movement, hardly heroic but perfectly natural, he had seized his belt and his revolver which had been thrown on the table, when he remembered my presence:

'Ah, Captain. Since you are here, counter-attack!'

'But . . . in which direction, sir?'

'Counter-attack, straight in front of you!'

'Yes, sir.'

I hurried up the steps in order to regroup my men and counter-attack northwards, in the direction of the Ourcq. In a few minutes the company had formed two lines of riflemen and, before the eyes of the sergeant-major who had returned to his observation post at the entrance to the cellar, we made a first rush forward. I must admit that when I saw my two lines twenty yards apart begin to advance, the men at intervals of four paces, I felt a thrill of pride. This was the result of my long efforts during the winter spent on taking my company in hand and forging it anew. Never more than on that day have I had the feeling of having played a personal and effective part in manipulating human clay. We set off, indeed, as if we were on manœuvres, but there was one slight detail that did not conform with regulations: the officers of the company were all three in the front line. Automatically, without conferring with one another, we were setting an example. This is the leader's A.B.C.

We made a second rush forward. As we started on our third rush I saw that two of my men on the left remained stretched out on the ground. They had just been killed. 'Down, men, down!' I ordered, and observed the terrain. The company had an excellent field of fire before it, rolling down on a gentle slope towards the Ourcq. I defied the Germans to move through it. As for their tank—we had seen only one—it appeared to want to remain in the shelter of the tree under which it was standing. At that moment Robin joined me, his face strangely contracted: he had just received a bullet in the arm. I handed over command to my 2nd Lieutenant and returned to report to the Major. The stout sergeant-major watched me go past, in, it seemed, quite a different manner. I explained the situation in a few words and returned to my position. That same evening we were relieved and went back to join our regiment.

An inexperienced officer newly arrived at the

front, with his head full of rules and theories, would probably have thought that he ought to continue his advance and have half of his men killed for nothing. But by 1918 we had had enough experience of the realities of the battle-field to check our losses in time. The Americans, who had just entered the front line near by at Château-Thierry, naturally did not have this experience, and one knows what enormous losses they suffered during the few months in which they took an active part.

This counter-attack was to have an unexpected epilogue, as far as I was concerned. Some ten days later, while we were in reserve behind Mosloy, I saw Colonel Roubert, Divisional Infantry Commander, drive up in his motor-car. The Colonel, who was Acting Brigadier, had the reputation for being a difficult man and always dissatisfied. It was therefore with some trepidation that I saw him arrive. My company, as I have already said, was looked down on by everyone, we were intruders from a disbanded regiment, 'the odds and ends' as my grandmother used to say of her daughters-in-law. What now? What was my company to be upbraided for this time? Certainly something serious since the Divisional Infantry Commander himself had come over.

Roubert approached me with a severe look in his eye and said:

'Captain, I am pleased to offer you my congratulations. Major Y, Battalion Commander of the 121st, has sent in an excellent report on the conduct of your company on 3rd June. This report was forwarded to us through the 2nd Cavalry Corps to which our division is at present attached. I invite you to forward recommenda-

148

tions for any of your men to be mentioned in orders.'

I was dumbfounded. So this fine Major of the 121st had gone to the trouble to praise troops who were not his and in whom he was not in any way personally interested. This fact must be unique in military history. Looking back, I was grateful to the stout sergeant-major who had seemed so hostile, yet who, having witnessed my counter-attack, must have supplied his Commanding Officer with the details for his report.

Chance had therefore enabled my company, which had been treated as a pariah in our new regiment, to show its mettle while it was lost in another division. Thanks to this, Colonel Roubert had had the satisfaction of receiving the congratulations of the Cavalry Corps, an amazing feat for an infantryman. My company was immediately established in the regiment's esteem. It was a beautiful revenge.

The revenge was even more complete for the very day of the counter-attack I had been told to take over command of the battalion in place of the Major who did not like me and whom I liked even less, and who had just been wounded and sent to the rear. When I reached Battalion Headquarters I asked my runner, who was always there, what had happened. In the rough outspoken manner of the men of the Vendée he replied:

'The bloody bastard got a little bit of splinter in his hand and off he went at once. The son of a bitch, that wouldn't have been enough to stop my son from going to school!'

For the French soldier sees through everything, and he is almost infallible in his judgement of his officers.

XX

DEPARTURE FROM THE FRONT

ONE day in March or April our Commanding Officer had been asked to send in a return with the names of all officers with a knowledge of English. I had given in my name without paying much attention to what seemed to me just another example of red tape. We had had to send in so many returns, some of them simply marked 'nil'. We were badgered with forms even in the front line and in the midst of the fighting. I did not then know that this simple return was to alter my fate and perhaps even save my life.

In the early days of June the German offensive had been halted and the front became stable. In the front line our lives were passed nestling in our separate shell-holes with no continuous trenches, and so we had to wait until night had fallen before we could move around and receive our rations. One night at the beginning of July, I was in the shell-hole which served as my Headquarters and I was gloomily thinking that, without realizing it, I had just had my twenty-fifth birthday—but does a man under suspended sentence of death celebrate his birthday?—when a new Battalion Commander turned up to take over. We introduced ourselves, and shaking me by the hand he said that he regretted that he did not know me better, but I had been posted to the American Forces as an information officer and that I was to leave that night for the rear.

Although it was pitch dark I was completely dazzled by this news. I immediately realized that for me the war was over, I had come through, I was suddenly free of the cruel anguish which had weighed on me for three and a half years, I was no more to be haunted by the spectre of death which had obsessed me as it obsesses old men.

Man is a strange animal. As I had only a few hours left at the front, I should logically have tried to reduce to a minimum the risks of these last moments and be doubly careful to avoid the bullet or the shell-burst which could put an end to my intoxicating hopes. But a fig for logic! I was gay and light-hearted and I felt that I was invulnerable. I took the new Commander on a tour of the sector, ignoring the bursts of machine-gun fire and the shells which were pounding the ground—though it is true that most of them passed over our heads. Having reached the right flank of my sector I took leave of him, after entrusting him to the care of the section leader of the next company. Before I left I gave him some words of warning:

'Do be careful. There's more danger to be expected here from the French than from the Germans. Do not go out into no-man's-land without making sure first that all your sentries have been warned, for we're in a sector where the men are at the end of their tether and inclined to be nervous, and they'll fire at anything they see moving. Do be careful!'

The Major, who had just come from the General Staff, thanked me condescendingly, as if to let me know that he had no need of my advice. I learnt

151

later that shortly afterwards he had been mortally wounded by one of our own men who had not been warned that he was making his rounds—a cruel penalty for fate to inflict on this brilliant staff-officer for not having wished to listen to the advice of a humble regimental officer.

I had to make my farewells to my company, but how was I to do so? It was of course quite impossible to assemble them together, nor could I visit all the men dispersed in their individual shell-holes, so I decided to limit myself to shaking hands with each of my sergeants, the king-pins of the company. I was filled with a mixture of pride and remorse on seeing what my departure meant to them. I can still see one of them who, up to the moment when our old regiment was disbanded, had spent the entire campaign in the supply lines and was now up at the front for the first time. I asked him how he was getting on in his new duties. He answered in a disheartened voice, death in his soul and eyes, desperate at having lost his sheltered position. I learnt later that he had been killed a week after I had left.

And I also remember Breucq, a rough miner from the north, an excellent soldier but terrible when he had been drinking. (One day when we were in billets he decided to let fly with his Lewis gun. By some miracle no one was hurt. He had to be strapped hand and foot before he could be brought to reason.) Breucq, who was sitting in his shell-hole as I went by, had already learnt that I was leaving by way of the bush telegraph which still worked even among men dispersed in the front line.

'So you're leaving us, sir?' he said. 'It's not right, sir, it's not right.'

I had a small twinge of remorse. No, it was not right to leave the company alongside whom I had fought for three and a half years. All I could say, as I shook his hand, was, 'What can one do, it's orders.'

But I had a sense of uneasiness at leaving them, and I was smitten with remorse later when I learnt that a fortnight after my departure the company had suffered terribly and that Breucq was among the dead. And with mixed feelings, which combined concern with a certain amount of complacency, I told myself that if I had been there things would have turned out differently.

After saying good-bye to my company I left for the rear. While my orderly and I were going past batteries of 75s, profiting from the calm that always preceded the dawn—at that hour the gunners on both sides must have been dead tired—I thought of what had happened to me. I had been ordered back from the front to go and help the new American Forces, I had escaped from the thousand dangers which could have still awaited me before the end came—the end which no one would have predicted for the forthcoming November—and all because, when I was ten years old and was about to enter the lowest form at school, I had to take either English or German as a living language and my father had chosen English on my behalf, due to the fact that at Rochefort, where I was brought up, most of my fellow-pupils hoped to enter the Naval College and therefore did English. On that day my father, without realizing it, had made a decision which was to affect the course of my life.

As I arrived at Mareuil-sur-Ourcq where our baggage train lay and where I was to pick up my uniform-case, I ran into a small detachment of the American Forces—some twenty strapping great fellows, sappers, admirably turned out with brand-new equipment, who gave the impression of unruffled strength. We knew that great battalions of men were arriving from the United States every day, at Le Havre, Brest, Saint-Nazaire and Bordeaux, and this small group was for me a symbol of the reinforcements that we were going to receive and boosted my hope and confidence. With the help of these fresh troops we were sure of winning. I have never forgotten this brief moment of exaltation, and I have always retained a deep sense of gratitude for those who helped us in our moment of need and turned the scales in our favour, and I have always resented those Frenchman who so easily forget how the Americans came to our rescue. It was not France's least error after the war to imagine that she had fought alone, invoking the one and a half million dead that she had lost. This excess of patriotism brought with it its own betrayal, and went a long way to prepare the disaster of 1940.